Trails of the
Wild Cabinets

Dennis Nicholls

KEOKEE
BOOKS

Keokee Books is an imprint of Keokee Co. Publishing, Inc.

Published by:

Keokee Co. Publishing, Inc.

P.O. Box 722

Sandpoint, ID 83864

(208) 263-3573

www.keokeebooks.com

ISBN 1-879628-21-8

Foreword

A tip of the (size 4) hat to Straight-up Joe

We have a theory, concocted and refined in the heart of the Cabinets, first with friend Jeff Pennick, and later, Dennis Nicholls, this book's author. We suppose he who built the first trails in those parts had 24-inch thighs, a 54-inch chest, a size 4 hat and no knowledge of switchbacks. What we named him is unprintable, so I'll call him "Straight-up Joe."

In spite of Joe's lack of consideration for us who would follow him, his trails lead through some most remarkable places, and traveling them with Dennis Nicholls makes them even more interesting. I can think of no one of his gender that makes better company on a trek to the high country. But I don't let him get in front.

Dennis has a larger hat size than Straight-up but the same legs and lungs. He burns ordinary hikers out in the first half-day, should he be in the lead. He's also insane. If you crawl with him along the top of Vimy Ridge at 7,500 feet in a blizzard in early April, with 300-foot drops on both sides, he will turn to you and shout over the 50-knot wind, "Isn't this fun?" with the glee of a 10-year-old at Disneyland.

As you use this guide to find some of the remarkable places in the wild Cabinets, remember that if Dennis says he's been there, he has, and you can trust him when he tells you what to expect and how to find the trail. It's probably not quite as good as having him along in person, but it might be better than running the risk of letting him get in front.

– M.R. "Sandy" Compton Jr.
Heron, Montana

The Cabinet Mountain Range
of northwestern Montana and northern Idaho

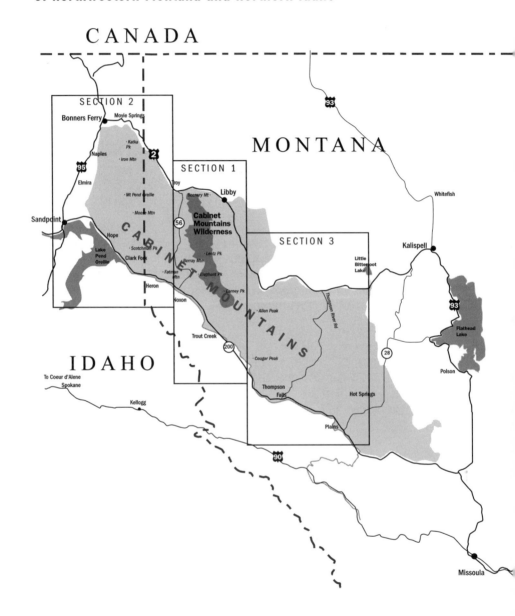

CANADA

SECTION 2

Bonners Ferry · Moyie Springs

· Katka Pk

Naples

· Iron Mtn

95

Elmira

Sandpoint

Hope

Lake Pend Orielle

Clark Fork

Heron

Troy

· Mt Pend Oreille

· Moose Mtn

CABINET

· Scotchman Pk

· Berray Mtn

· Fatman Mtn

Noxon

Trout Creek

MONTANA

93

SECTION 1

· Scenery Mt · Libby

Cabinet Mountains Wilderness

56

· Lentz Pk

· Elephant Pk

· Carney Pk

MOUNTAINS

· Allen Peak

200

· Cougar Peak

Thompson Falls

SECTION 3

Little Bitteroot Lake

Thompson River Rd

Hot Springs

Plains

90

Whitefish

Kalispell

93

Flathead Lake

Polson

28

IDAHO

To Coeur d'Alene
Spokane

Kellogg

Missoula

Contents

Section I. Cabinet Mountains Wilderness

Appendices

Acknowledgements _ _ _ _

This is the first book I have written, and I hope it is not the last because I have come to realize it takes quite an effort on the part of a lot of really cool people to put something like this together. I want to express my deepest appreciation to Chris Bessler, the publisher and whose idea this book was; Laura White, without whose skills at mapmaking and design this book would not have made it to the printer (and thanks for the granola and orange slices); Billie Jean Plaster, a terrific editor for whom I always write too many words; the Forest Service trails people whose job it is to keep these trails open – Les Raynor in Trout Creek, Mark Childress in Plains, Jon Jeresek in Libby, Mark Mason in Troy, Mary Ann Hamilton in Sandpoint and Pat Hart in Bonners Ferry; and a flashback special thanks goes to a man I have not seen in years, but who took me hiking in the Blue Ridge Mountains when I was a kid and taught me much of what I know about back-packing, Jerry Hogan. I hope, in your old age, Jerry, you are still on the trail from time to time because I would love to cross paths with you again someday.

– Dennis Nicholls

Introduction

Between Hope and Paradise

There was a time when I would walk a thousand miles in a summer, every summer. Some of the walking I did because my work required it. But on days when I wasn't working in the woods, I was in the woods anyway hiking to places I had never been or revisiting favorite spots in hopes the fish were still biting, or to see if a band of elk had passed through or if a bear knew of the same huckleberry patch I did. Rain or shine, there was no place I'd rather be than on a trail in this paradise of peaks and valleys sculpted by glaciers, busting my way through the undergrowth to some secret enclave deep in the mountains. I would walk and walk and the miles would add up, and the majesty of the country I discovered would, without fail, instill a new sense of delight inside me.

My knees won't allow that kind of mileage now, but if I don't get out and hike absolutely as far as I can push myself, I feel as though I cheat myself out of one of the great pleasures in life: the solitude of wilderness.

Fortunately, I live close to vast expanses of country wilder than anything I ever imagined as a child. My brothers and I always dreamed of living in the mountains; whether it was the Blue Ridge, the Alleghenies, the Great Smokies or the Rockies, it didn't matter. Yet, as a young boy with a blossoming love for the outdoors, it was hard for me to imagine that dream coming true, growing up in a big Eastern city like I did.

The author, left, and his oldest brother, Archie, on top of Engle Peak

My boyhood dreams did come true, however, and with them have come worn-out boots and calloused feet from the thousands of miles they have carried me through the Northern Rockies.

When my father agreed I could go to college in Montana, I believe he thought I would return to Virginia. Except for occasional visits, though, I haven't. I settled down in the west end of the state and for more than 25 years I have explored a few of Montana's wilderness gems. My stand-alone favorite has been the Cabinet Mountains.

I live on the southwest edge of the Cabinets, which stretch for more than a hundred miles from Hope, Idaho to Paradise, Montana. I have always relished the notion that I live in a magical land somewhere between hope and paradise. Not many other people have found this slice of heaven tucked into a fold of the countryside between the Purcell Trench and the Continental Divide. It is not as well known as other mountain ranges closer to more people, and that's all right by me. I have become jealous for the Cabinets and wince when I find others on the same trail as I; yet, here I am writing a guide to hiking in this remote corner of Montana. I guess that is because I enjoy showing off my part of the Rocky Mountains to visitors and friends. I see it as a way to help preserve what is left of the wildness here. Introducing new folks to the wonders of the Cabinets, I hope, will help build a constituency for protecting the glaciated peaks, the dark cedar forests and the wild creatures that still inhabit them.

If you find satisfaction in hiking and scrambling and clawing your way hand over foot to dizzying heights where the clouds are often below your feet; if you enjoy the serenity of a clear blue mountain lake; if ancient trees whispering secrets to the wind sends shivers down your spine, then I believe the Cabinet Mountains would be more than happy to make your acquaintance.

The Cabinets are easier to find than you might think. Just begin searching for that magical land somewhere between Hope and Paradise.

— Dennis Nicholls
Noxon, Montana
Spring 2003

About this Guide

When thinking about going on a hike, for a mountain bike ride or out on horseback, what is one of the first things you do? You look for information about the area you want to explore. *Trails of the Wild Cabinets* hopefully contains enough information, including where to go for more information, about the Cabinet Mountains that you will want to explore these mountains for yourself. This is not an exhaustive guide. There are easily twice as many trails in the Cabinets as are mentioned here, but this guide covers most of the best trails just enough to whet your appetite. It is a great place to start becoming familiar with this range of mountains in northwest Montana and northern Idaho.

The primary focus of this guide is on hiking, but every trail discussed here is open to horses. Horsemen should judge for themselves the suitability of these trails for horseback rides. Check for restrictions regarding livestock, particularly near wilderness lakes. Mountain bikes are somewhat more restricted than horses and hikers – they are not allowed in the Cabinet Mountains Wilderness. All trails outside the wilderness, however, are open to mountain bikes and, again, mountain bikers should judge for themselves the suitability of any of these trails for their form of recreation. A guide to the use of these trails by mountain bikes can be found toward the back of this book, beginning on page 152.

A lot of trailheads are clearly marked and easy to find, but many are poorly signed, not signed at all, obscure and difficult to locate. The directions to trailheads in this book are fairly precise, but it always helps to refer to detailed maps and to ask assistance from trails people with the U.S. Forest Service. Some trailheads are scheduled for upgrades in the near future or even relocation. If you have problems with finding where to embark on a hike, it never hurts to put a plug in for better signage with the district responsible for trail maintenance.

There is a lot of mixed ownership in this range. Most trails are on public land, but some start or pass through private and/or corporate lands for which legal easements or permission from landowners has been obtained, so always respect private property.

The details offered in these pages about each hike comes from maps, signs, Forest Service booklets or pamphlets, conversations with others and, most of all, the author's own hiking experiences. Distances and elevation gains are usually rounded off to the nearest mile or hundred feet. For the most part, you can expect these hikes to be over 4 miles one way and seldom less than 2,000 vertical feet in elevation gained, but the majority of the trails are in good or excellent condition.

If you are looking for a particular kind of experience when exploring the Cabinets, you might find it beneficial to refer to the Features Chart, beginning on page 14, a few pages behind this section. It is a handy quick reference on where to find waterfalls, forest fire lookouts, which hikes have elements of historical significance, and other information that can help you select a hike that most interests you.

Quantifying the level of difficulty is based on three criteria: distance, elevation gained and condition of trail. It is also subjective and depends largely on each hiker's abilities. The author assumes most people utilizing this guide have done some hiking and are in reasonably good health. That would make most of these hikes pretty easy to somewhat difficult. Each person should be aware of their limitations and judge for themselves just how hard a hike might be based on the information you will find in this guide and perhaps from talking to others who have made the hike.

The level of difficulty for the hikes described in this book is expressed in "The Sweat Index." Each rating is defined in the table below.

The Sweat Index: Level of Difficulty

1. Easy: No sweat, an easy hike that practically anyone of any ability can do. Example: Ross Creek Nature Trail No. 405.

2. Moderate: A hike that will probably make you breathe heavy and cause you to break a sweat, but you will think it was a piece of cake. Example: Gem Lake Trail No. 554.

3. Difficult: Sweating profusely during the day, you will likely want to go to bed early tonight, weary from a pleasant day in the mountains. Example: 20 Odd Peak Trail No. 898.

4. Strenuous: The kind of hike that will more than likely test your endurance and tax your strength, but at the end of the day you may well wipe the salty sweat stinging your eyes and exclaim, "That was a dandy!" Example: William Grambauer Mountain Trail No. 319.

Precautions

There are common factors to always be aware of when hiking, no matter the destination. In the Cabinet Mountains, as for hiking in any mountainous terrain, here are some things to watch out for:

- Sunburn – use sunscreen or wear clothing that covers exposed skin, including hats and/or sunglasses to shield your eyes.

- Snow blindness – wear sunglasses when hiking in snow on bright days.

- Extreme weather conditions any time of the year – always pack sufficient extra clothing and dress in layers.

- Hypothermia – don't sweat so much that you lose body heat faster than your body can replace it; that is very dangerous.

- Obstacles in the trail – watch for rocks, roots, stobs, limbs, logs and other hazards that can trip you up or make you fall, especially when damp and slippery.

- Insects – the Cabinets are a wet mountain range and breed lots of biting and stinging insects; wear appropriate clothing and have insect repellent handy, or be ready to run screaming through the forest in maniacal panic.

- Wildlife – hikers, hunters, fishermen and other outdoors enthusiasts are not the only creatures in these mountains. Always give wild animals a wide berth or leave an area entirely if any animals you encounter don't leave; remember, you are the visitor and the animals live here.

- The Cabinet Mountains harbor a lot of black bears and a few grizzly bears. Familiarize yourself with techniques on how to hike and camp safely in bear habitat.

- Dehydration – it's simple: don't drink enough water, you dehydrate, and that is bad; always drink plenty of water when hiking any time of the year.

- Availability of Water – with upwards of 100 inches of precipitation annually in the Cabinets, you can expect to find water in lots of places, but it is always wisest to filter it, boil it or otherwise treat it before drinking; nothing is worse than a case of giardia.

- Others on the trail – it is not unusual to hike for miles or even days in the Cabinets without seeing another soul, but sooner or later you will encounter someone else on foot, perhaps on a mountain bike or on horse-back. Courtesy and politeness will always make such encounters more enjoyable.

From time to time you may wonder about the names of places you are hiking to. As you explore and become more familiar with the Cabinets, you will notice some unusual names (Hunt Girl Creek and Found Girl Creek – there has got to be a good story there); some mundane names (Middle Mountain); quite a few repetitive names (Miller Creek); and an occasional politically incorrect name (Squaw Peak).

An effort has been under way to rename features that carry the "squaw" label because of its offensive nature. In the Cabinets there are at least three landmarks identified by that word: Squaw Peak north of Heron, and Squaw Pass and Squaw Creek, both north of Thompson Falls. New names for these places have not yet been adopted.

Hiking guides are useful tools, but that is all they are – tools. The greatest sense of satisfaction in the Great Outdoors is experienced when exploring places and making discoveries for yourself. Please use this guide to get started, perhaps pointing you in a certain direction, and then go see the Cabinet Mountains with your own eyes and hike the trails on your own two feet. You will likely break a sweat, find your strength drained and your endurance challenged, but I bet at the end of the trail, in the twilight of the waning day, you will exclaim, "That was a dandy!"

Trails of the Wild Cabinets Features Chart

Many people like to plan hikes for particular reasons: They want to go to a mountaintop, visit a lake, picnic by a waterfall, increase the likelihood of seeing wildlife. There are as many reasons for hiking as there are hikers. This section of *Trails of the Wild Cabinets* offers a quick glance at the features that can be found along many of the trails described in this book. These features are in the following categories:

- Waterfall – identifies significant waterfalls located along or near a trail.

- Wildlife – many species of wildlife inhabit the Cabinets, but some hikes offer special opportunities at viewing wildlife such as moose or mountain goats.

- Lake – the majority of the trails covered in this book provide access to high mountain lakes.

- Mountaintop – if the trail does not go to a lake, then it likely climbs to the summit of a high peak; and sometimes it does both.

- Historical – a few trails harbor sites of historical significance, such as old trappers' cabins or mining sites.

- Lookout – some mountain tops have forest fire lookout towers on them, a few of which are still manned, though most are now abandoned and either falling into disrepair, or in a few cases, are being preserved as historical sites.

- Old Growth – because the Cabinets are home to fast-growing forests, the timber industry has thrived here for over a hundred years; however, some spectacular stands of old-growth forests still remain, as well as some remarkable individual trees that are worth mentioning.

- Wildfire – Forest fires play a major role in the shaping of the environment and there are areas of significant burns in the past 10 years that offer excellent opportunity for viewing and studying the effects of wildfire.

- Connector Trail – a few trails do not access specific destinations themselves; instead they provide a connection between other trails and destinations a hiker may be headed for.

An X in the columns beside the trail number indicates the features present somewhere along that trail. This is not necessarily an all-inclusive list of features to be found along the trails of the Cabinet Mountains, but it is a good place to start when planning to hike to a specific destination.

Cabinet Mountain Wilderness

The North End: William Grambauer Mountain to Flower Creek

Trail Name & No.	Length	One Way	Waterfall	Wildlife	Lake	Mountaintop	Historical	Lookout	Old Growth	Wildfire	Connector Trail
William Grambauer Mtn. Trail No. 319	7 mi					X			X		
Scenery Mountain Trail No. 649	5 mi					X	X	X	X		
Cedar Lakes Trail No. 141	5 mi				X				X		
Taylor Peak Trail No. 320	8 mi					X			X		
Dome Mountain Trail No. 360	7 mi				X	X					X
Minor Lake Trail No. 317	4 mi				X						X
Parmenter Creek Trail No. 140	8 mi				X						
Flower Creek/Sky Lakes Trail No. 137	6 mi				X				X		
Hanging Valley Trail No. 135	3 mi				X						

The Central CMW: Granite Creek to Rock Lake

Trail Name & No.	Length	One Way	Waterfall	Wildlife	Lake	Mountaintop	Historical	Lookout	Old Growth	Wildfire	Connector Trail
Crowell Creek Trail No. 326	3 mi	X									
North Fork Bull River Trail No. 972	4 mi	X		X							
Middle Fork Bull River Trail No. 978	7 mi	X									
Little Ibex Lake Trail No. 980	2 mi				X						
Granite Lake Trail No. 136	6 mi	X			X				X		
Leigh Lake Trail No. 132	2 mi	X			X				X		
Dad Peak Trail No. 966	5 mi		X			X			X	X	
St. Paul Lake Trail No. 646	4 mi	X			X				X		
Moran Basin Trail No. 993	13 mi				X						
Rock Lake Trail No. 935	4 mi	X	X		X		X				
Trail to Cliff Lake	1 mi		X		X						
Berray Mountain West Trail No. 967	5 mi		X			X	X	X			
Berray Mountain Trail No. 1028	2 mi					X	X	X			

The South End: Wanless Lake to Baree Lake

Trail Name & No.	Length	One Way	Waterfall	Wildlife	Lake	Mountaintop	Historical	Lookout	Old Growth	Wildfire	Connector Trail
Engle Lake Trail No. 932	4 mi				X						
Engle Peak Trail No. 926	6 mi					X					
Wanless Lake Trail No. 924	9 mi	X			X						
Swamp Creek Trail No. 912	13 mi	X			X						
Bramlet Lake Trail No. 658	2 mi				X		X				
Geiger Lakes Trail No. 656	4 mi				X						
Cabinet Divide Trail No. 360	14 mi					X					X
Iron Meadow Trail No. 113	3 mi								X		
Bear Lakes Trail No. 531	3 mi				X						
Baree Lake Trail No. 489	4 mi				X		X				
Divide Cutoff Trail No. 63	3 mi				X				X		X

The West Cabinets

Katka-Boulder

Trail Name & No.	Length	One Way	Waterfall	Wildlife	Lake	Mountaintop	Historical	Lookout	Old Growth	Wildfire	Connector Trail
Katka Peak Trail No. 182	4 mi					X					
McGinty Ridge Trail No. 143	4 mi					X					
Iron Mountain Trail No. 180	5 mi					X					
Buck Mountain Trail No. 176	8 mi					X					
East Fork Boulder Creek Trail No. 136	8 mi					X			X		
Timber Mountain Trail No. 51	20 mi				X	X					
Kelly Pass Trail No. 155	3 mi					X					X

Trail Name & No.	One Way	Waterfall	Wildlife	Lake	Mountaintop	Historical	Lookout	Old Growth	Wildfire	Connector Trail
Orville Heath Trail No. 54	3 mi				X					X
North Callahan Trail No. 548	4 mi							X		X
Pend Oreille Divide										
Pend Oreille Divide Trail No. 67	15 mi	X			X					
Lake Darling Trail No. 52	2 mi	X	X							
Gem Lake Trail No. 554	2 mi		X							
Moose Lake Trail No. 237	2 mi	X	X							
Blacktail Lake Trail No. 24	3 mi	X	X							
Lake Estelle Trail No. 36	3 mi	X	X							
Bee Top-Round Top No. 120	19 mi				X					
Bee Top Trail No. 63	3 mi				X					
Strong Creek Trail No. 444	5 mi				X					
Scotchman Peaks										
Little Spar Lake Trail No. 143	4 mi	X	X							
Ross Creek Trail No. 405	1 mi					X		X		
Pillick Ridge Trail No. 1036	11 mi				X	X	X	X		
Star Gulch Trail No. 1016	7 mi				X					X
Napoleon Gulch Trail No. 1035	9 mi				X	X				X
Big Eddy Trail No. 998	4 mi				X	X	X			
Blacktail Creek Trail No. 997	2 mi									
Hamilton Gulch Trail No. 1019	3 mi									
Scotchman Peak Trail No. 65	4 mi				X	X				
East Fork Peak Trail No. 563	3 mi				X	X				

The Southern Cabinets

Vermilion-Fisher River

Trail Name & No.	One Way	Waterfall	Wildlife	Lake	Mountaintop	Historical	Lookout	Old Growth	Wildfire	Connector Trail
20 Odd Peak Trail No. 898	4 mi				X	X				
Canyon Peak Trail No. 903	3 mi				X					
Allen Peak Trail No. 293	2 mi				X					
Moose Peak Trail No. 877	3 mi		X		X					
Elk Lake Trail No. 882	1 mi			X						
Elk Mountain Trail No. 861	3 mi				X					
Cataract Creek Trail No. 847	7 mi				X					
Water Hill Trail No. 845	12 mi				X					
Vermilion Seven-Point Trail No. 528	6 mi				X					
Trail to Vermilion Falls	100 yd	X								
Cabinet Divide Trail No. 360	14 mi	X			X					X

Cabinet Lakes-Thompson River

Trail Name & No.	One Way	Waterfall	Wildlife	Lake	Mountaintop	Historical	Lookout	Old Growth	Wildfire	Connector Trail
Winniemuck Creek Trail No. 506	6 mi	X	X							
Vermilion-Headley Trail No. 528	4 mi				X					
Thompson-Headley Trail No. 450	5 mi	X	X		X			X		
Cabin Lake Trail No. 459	3 mi		X					X		
South Four Lakes Creek Trail No. 460	3 mi			X						
Big Spruce Creek Trail No. 1102	4 mi			X						
Honeymoon Creek Trail No. 469	4 mi			X						
Sundance Ridge Trail No. 433	14 mi				X	X	X			
Munson Creek Trail No. 372	6 mi	X			X	X	X		X	
Baldy National Recreation Trail No. 340	3 mi			X	X	X				

Discovering the Cabinet Mountains

Elmira Peak, 3,852 feet. Two Tail Peak, 3,949 feet. Any idea what they might have in common? Well, kind of the same thing as Communion Butte (3,483 feet) and Sonyok Mountain (5,580 feet). Elmira and Two Tail are both near Bonners Ferry, Idaho, and represent the westernmost and northernmost named summits in the Cabinet Mountains. Communion Butte and Sonyok are both on the Flathead Indian Reservation near Dixon, Montana, and represent the easternmost and southernmost named summits in the Cabinets. The two mountains in northern Idaho are roughly 150 miles from those two in Montana.

South Fork of Ross Creek Falls

Ask anyone where the Cabinet Mountains are and they will either shrug their shoulders and say, "Don't know," or they will likely refer to a cluster of peaks south and west of Libby, Montana, and exclaim, "Those are the Cabinets." They would not be wrong, of course, but few people – even those who love this range the most – are aware that the Cabinets sprawl across such an immense distance.

Boundaries

Surrounding the Cabinet Mountain Range are five other mountain ranges that are likely as little known as the Cabinets. To the west in Idaho and Washington and extending north into Canada are the Selkirks; in the extreme northeast corner of Idaho, northwest Montana and stretching into Canada are the Purcells; the Salish Mountains, a small range entirely located in Montana, flank the Cabinets to the northeast; and straddling the Idaho-Montana border along the southwest edge of the Cabinets lie the northernmost part of the Bitterroots, an immense chain of mountains sprawling over 300 miles from Lake Pend Oreille to Monida Pass.

A complex array of ownership and jurisdictions interlock across the 2 million acres encompassed by the Cabinet Mountains. They spread into two states, five counties, an Indian Reservation, three National Forests and seven ranger districts. Nearly two-thirds of this landscape belongs to the public; a chunk in the southeast end is part of all that is left of the territorial homeland of the Salish and Kootenai tribes; tens of thousands of acres are managed by timber, mining and railroad corporations; and the rest – less than 10 percent – is in private hands.

The Cabinet Mountains form a range fairly easy to define. Three major rivers and several smaller ones mark its boundaries. The farthest upstream one can go and still be on the edge of the Cabinets would be at Little Bitterroot Lake, which rests at the northeastern corner of this range near Marion, Montana. At 3,903 feet above sea level, it is downstream from here along every border of the Cabinets.

The Little Bitterroot River flows south out of this lake through Camas Prairie and joins the Flathead River between The Big Bend and The Oxbow, not far downstream from Kerr Dam. At this point the Flathead is already a large river as it drains the west side of Glacier National Park, much of the Bob Marshall Wilderness complex and has just departed the largest natural freshwater lake west of the Mississippi – Flathead Lake.

Near Paradise, Montana, the Flathead flows into the smaller Clark's Fork of the Columbia, which is usually called the Clark Fork River. From here the Clark Fork flows in a northwesterly direction along the southwest edge of the Cabinets for nearly 100 miles. Just below Clark Fork, Idaho, the largest river system in Montana by volume empties its gargantuan current into Idaho's largest lake, Lake Pend Oreille (pronounced Pon-duh-ray). The elevation at the Clark Fork delta is 2,062 feet.

It is nearly 180 miles by water from Little Bitterroot Lake to Lake Pend Oreille with an elevation loss of 1,841 feet, or an average of 10 feet per mile.

From Little Bitterroot Lake west to Sedlak Park, an edge of the Cabinet Mountains follows the Thompson Chain of Lakes, a series of a dozen lakes strung like pearls on a necklace from McGregor Lake to Loon Lake. This is the headwaters area for the Thompson River, the largest interior drainage in this range.

At Sedlak Park the Pleasant Valley Fisher River and Silver Butte Fisher River meet and flows north as the Fisher River to its confluence with the Kootenai River about 14 miles east of Libby, Montana. From here the Kootenai forms the northeast boundary of the Cabinets all the way to Bonners Ferry, Idaho, situated on the south shore of the river at an elevation of 1,777 feet. Where the Kootenai leaves Montana is the lowest elevation anywhere in that state.

It is nearly 130 miles from Little Bitterroot Lake to Bonners Ferry with an elevation loss of 2,123 feet, or an average of about 16 feet per mile.

The west side of the Cabinets is delineated by the Purcell Trench, down which the continental ice sheet last made its advance approximately 12,000 years ago. Between Bonners Ferry on the Kootenai River and the town of Hope, Idaho, on Lake Pend Oreille, this part of the Purcell Trench is drained by Deep Creek flowing north out of McArthur Lake and the Pack River, which flows southeast into Lake Pend Oreille. The divide separating these two drainages is close to the Elmira Store, just a mile or so southwest of Elmira Peak, the westernmost named summit in the Cabinets.

Geology

In a 1963 report authored by F.A. Crowley about the mines and minerals of Sanders County, Crowley wrote, "Sanders County can be likened to a person whose childhood was eventful, whose middle age was wasted, and whose predominant characteristics were shaped late in life."

The geographic area now known as the Cabinet Mountains and the lower Clark Fork River Valley were conceived 600 million years ago when thousands of feet of sediments were deposited over millions of years in a vast shallow sea. Geologically, these sediments today are identified as the Belt Series. For almost half a billion years, the Belt Series deposits were lifted, folded and shaped by geologic forces that created the mountain range. Then during the Mesozoic Era more than 13 million centuries ago, granite was intruded in parts of the sedimentary layers of the Belt Series. While exposed granite is not common in the Cabinet Mountains, the Selkirk Range immediately to the west is comprised almost entirely of granite.

The headwall of the Middle Fork of Ross Creek

Of greater significance to the shaping of the Cabinets was the magnificent Cordilleran Ice Sheet that descended from the north during the Wisconsin Stage of the Pleistocene period of glaciation. After the ominous beginnings of small glaciers in the high mountains, a massive surge of glacial ice advanced across northwestern Montana from Canada. The ice sheet's advance largely halted north and east of the Clark Fork valley, but perhaps most spectacular of all was the great wall of ice that moved down the Purcell Trench in Idaho. A lobe of that ice pushed upstream from present-day Lake Pend Oreille and created a 2,000-foot-high ice dam near Heron, Montana.

Over and over again for tens of thousands of years, it is thought this ice dam formed, broke and reformed in creating one of the largest bodies of freshwater ever known: Glacial Lake Missoula. Perhaps 12,000 years ago the ice dam broke for the last time, the ice retreated, and the massive flooding from Missoula, Montana to Portland, Oregon is the basis for one of the most incredible geologic events known to man.

Landscapes and Climate

During the millennia since the end of the Ice Age, the Cabinet Mountains have evolved into the region we know today. Encircled by the boundaries of this range are mountains that harbor an incredible variety of landscapes and habitats, from temperate rainforest to desert-like prairie. From the famous grove of ancient cedars at Ross Creek to the parched prickly pear cactus and grasslands of Camas Prairie, annual rainfall varies from more than 100 inches above the Bull River Valley to less than 10 inches near the small schoolhouse south of Markle Pass.

Snowfall varies as much as the rainfall does, from scarcely a foot of snow a year at Hot Springs, Montana to almost a dozen feet of snow at Noxon, Montana. It is safe to say much of the precipitation that falls in this region comes in the frozen form. Snow accumulation in the high country of the Cabinets is much greater than in the valleys and may well exceed 500 inches in a single winter.

Despite this fact, temperatures are moderate in this part of the Northern Rockies, as the climate is influenced more by Pacific air masses than by the colder, drier continental air masses that often slide south out of Canada farther east. One hundred degrees is not unheard of in late July or August, and the mercury can drop to 20 below zero at any time between late November and early February. But the lower Clark Fork Valley is not called the "banana belt" for no reason. During some winters the temperature may not go below zero at all, and it has been known to rain and remain cool all through the summer.

The wild card in being prepared for the weather is elevation: There is 7,000 vertical feet from the lowest point in the Cabinets at Bonners Ferry to the highest point atop Snowshoe Peak. Some years snow will fall at the highest elevations every month of the year, and old-timers still talk about snow in town on the Fourth of July way back when, and, in fact, that happened in the 1990s too.

The very fact that so much moisture falls on these mountains means the Cabinets boast some of the most lush vegetation anywhere in the Rockies. A dozen conifer species grow here, from cedar-hemlock forests in the valleys to the alpine larch and whitebark pine of the highest ridges. Myriads of hardwood trees and shrubs cloak many mountainsides with some of the gnarliest tangles imaginable. Tropical-like ferns and the dagger-like thorns of Devil's Club make some streamside environments look more like a rainforest than a Rocky Mountain canyon. Yet, across many upper slopes, more typical Rocky Mountain habitats sporting pinegrass, beargrass, huckleberry, grouse whortleberry and pachistima (or mountain myrtle) can be found.

That the climate is so variable across the breadth of the Cabinet Mountains is what makes them so unique and interesting.

Topography

The Cabinets are generally thought of as a collection of relatively low peaks. Of the more than 30 mountain ranges in Montana, this is one of only four that does not have any 9,000-foot peaks. Nonetheless, the Cabinets are impressive at least in part because of the low elevations at which its valleys are situated. For instance, where the north, middle and south forks of the Bull River come together and flow next to Montana Highway 56 is 2,356 feet. Just eight miles to the east, in full view of passersby, is the highest point in the Cabinets, Snowshoe Peak. It rises more than 6,300 feet from that viewpoint to its summit at 8,738 feet.

On the other side of the range sits Granite Lake in a steep-walled valley at 4,605 feet. Almost exactly a horizontal mile from the upper end of the lake is the second highest mountain in the range, A Peak, 8,634 feet, or more than 4,000 feet above the waters of Granite Lake. With a vertical-to-horizontal ratio of a thousand feet every quarter mile, this is one of the most precipitous escarpments anywhere in the Rocky Mountains.

Only one other peak exceeds 8,000 feet in the Cabinets – Bockman Peak at 8,174 feet. Those three high peaks (Snowshoe, A and Bockman) form the crown of the Cabinet Mountains and the federally protected wilderness of the same name. In fact, they are the highest peaks of any of the six ranges noted here south of the Canadian border until well south in the Bitterroots: Trapper Peak near Darby, Montana, tops 10,000 feet.

The Cabinet Mountains Wilderness Area (CMW) was first preserved as a Primitive Area in 1935. But with the passage of the 1964 Wilderness Act, 94,360 acres in the Cabinets became one of the first 10 designated wilderness areas in the country. Within the borders of this long, narrow wilderness are another 14 named peaks over 7,500 feet and 10 others that top 7,000 feet. It is known by those who know it best for its rugged beauty, its deep, forested valleys and the more than 100 lakes hidden away in glacially carved subalpine cirques.

Outside the wilderness, there is not another peak in the Cabinets over 7,500 feet, and only nine surpass 7,000 feet. Scotchman Peak, near Clark Fork, Idaho, at 7,009 feet is the highest point in the Idaho portion of the Cabinets. To the southeast, north of Plains, Montana, Baldy Mountain and Thompson Peak are the highest summits outside the wilderness at 7,464 and 7,460 feet, respectively.

Human History

It is likely people have inhabited this region since shortly after the ice left and the region became more hospitable to all kinds of creatures. Some scientists even speculate there may well have been humans here during the latter part of the Ice Age since this area was on the fringes of the ice. As the climate warmed and the land became overgrown with forests, the numbers of native inhabitants increased. However, much of the Cabinet Mountain Range remained inaccessible and remote because of its rugged terrain and dark, thick forests. To the east and north the Salish and Kootenai peoples thrived and to the west and south other native tribes such as the Coeur d'Alene and Kalispel flourished.

It wasn't until 1809 that the first European explorer set foot near the Cabinet Mountains. Though the Lewis and Clark Expedition had passed through western Montana a few years earlier, they never saw the Cabinets. David Thompson is credited as the first white man to wander along the banks of the Kootenai and Clark Fork rivers. He established a short-lived trading post near Hope, Idaho, and another a few miles west of Plains, Montana.

Once trappers discovered the richness of furs in this region, it did not take long for others to come here and discover other riches: timber and minerals.

The first railroad track was laid through the Clark Fork Valley in the 1880s, and for a hundred years there was a burst of development and growth that began to level off and change only in the past couple of decades. With the demise of mining and logging, the people now inhabiting the Cabinet Mountains are discovering anew a diversity of riches that are slowly redefining the economy of the region.

Communities and Access

Relatively few people live in or around the Cabinet Mountains today. The communities encircling this range include Clark Fork, Hope, Sandpoint, Elmira, Naples, Bonners Ferry and Moyie Springs in Idaho; and Troy, Libby, Lonepine, Hot Springs, Paradise, Plains, Thompson Falls, Trout Creek, Noxon and Heron in Montana. The Cabinets encompass approximately 3,000 square miles with perhaps 30,000 people living on its fringes. The nearest large population centers are Spokane, Washington, and Missoula, Montana.

The people here variously make their livings by working for some level of federal, state or local government; in the timber industry; in construction; in education; or they depend heavily on tourism. Real estate is hot because, in the big picture, there is so little private property in this region, and the abundant wildlife inhabiting these mountains brings in a lot of money from sportsmen. A growing industry in western Montana and northern Idaho is the proliferation of intervention programs for teens. One of the largest employers in Sanders County is a boarding school for troubled youth.

Only two paved highways bisect the Cabinets. Montana Highway 56 traverses the Bull River/Bull Lake valley between Noxon and Troy and connects Highway 200 and U.S. Highway 2. From Plains, Montana, Highway 28 climbs steeply to Rainbow Lake, passes by Hot Springs and carries on to Elmo on the western shore of Flathead Lake, connecting Highway 200 with U.S. Highway 93.

From these highways, access to the Cabinet Mountains is excellent. Because of the abundance of moisture, the mild climate and the longer-than-average Rocky Mountain growing season, trees grow big and fast here. Though fur trading is what brought the first explorers to this area, timber soon became king and a burgeoning industry quickly exploited the resource. Almost every major drainage and secondary drainage in the Cabinets has a road system. In recent years many of these roads have been closed or decommissioned to help provide security for wildlife and to minimize erosion, but a vast network of roads still offer easy access to what primitive and wilderness areas remain.

Wilderness and Wildlife

Within the range, the 94,000-plus acres of the CMW make up the only protected wilderness. Those acres represent about 5 percent of the landmass of the Cabinets. The U.S. Forest Service in the past has proposed adding about 35,000 acres to the CMW as well as creating a couple of other wilderness areas. The proposed Scotchman Peaks Wilderness would straddle the state line between Noxon, Montana, and Clark Fork, Idaho, and encompass 35,000 to 40,000 acres; the proposed Cube Iron-Silcox Wilderness would include about 30,000 acres north of Thompson Falls, Montana.

Others believe there is opportunity for preserving a great deal more acreage as wilderness throughout the range. For instance, a piece of legislation called the Northern Rockies Ecosystem

David Westerfeld, Sandy Compton and Mike Brown in the heart of the proposed Scotchman Peaks Wilderness

Protection Act has been before Congress for several years and proposes doubling the size of the CMW while adding another 370,000 acres throughout the range to the wilderness preservation system. Among the areas proffered for wilderness protection are 88,000 acres in the Scotchmans; more than 90,000 acres along the Pend Oreille Divide from Katka Peak to Lake Estelle; and over 60,000 acres in the Vermilion River and Silver Butte Fisher River drainages.

The need for preserving wild country, most everyone agrees, is primarily to provide secure habitat for the wild creatures inhabiting an area. When it comes to wildlife in the Cabinet Mountains, a rare situation exists. Perhaps all the animals indigenous to the Cabinets – those that were here when David Thompson first wandered along the Clark Fork River to establish Kullyspel House near Hope and then Saleesh House near Plains as trading posts in 1810 – are still here.

If anything, much of the wildlife in these mountains is probably doing better than they were 200 years ago. Journals from the expeditions undertaken by David Thompson and by Captains Meriwether Lewis and William Clark report big game animals were scarce in many parts of western Montana in the early 1800s. Today, whitetail deer and elk populations are as high as just about any time in known history; moose are abundant from swampy lowlands to high mountain slopes; bighorn sheep and mountain goats can be found on many of the craggy ridges of the Cabinets. Among ungulates, only mule deer are in a serious decline due to altered habitat and heavy hunting pressure.

So, because of healthy populations of ungulates and many small mammals like rabbits, squirrels, mice, voles and pikas, predators are commonplace as well. Though some species have been nearly eradicated and still hang in the balance, such as grizzly bears, others have made a resurgence, such as wolves. The newest wolf pack to occupy a home range in Montana was discovered in 2002 and has been called the Green Mountain Pack. It was last known to inhabit the McKay Creek drainage and adjacent wildlands north of Trout Creek. Wolves, like grizzlies, are on the federal Endangered Species List.

It is thought by wildlife biologists that perhaps fewer than 20 grizzly bears inhabit the Cabinet Mountains. The majority of those are concentrated around the wilderness area because of its secure and suitable habitat for these magnificent creatures. Though people seldom encounter grizzlies when hiking in the Cabinets, grizzlies frequent several of the more popular destinations hikers like to visit, such as Rock Lake, for instance. For the most part, grizzlies roam the high country and remote valleys as far from people as they can get. They dine on glacier lilies and other tuberous plants in the spring and feast on huckleberries in the fall. Being opportunistic feeders, they will also eat carrion and prey on fawns and elk calves. Other food sources, however, often draw them closer to human habitation, particularly if wild food sources are scarce.

There are significantly more black bears in the Cabinets than grizzlies, and they are found in all parts of the range. They can be equally as dangerous, particularly females with cubs. Though it is usually easy to tell the two species apart, people should know that black bears come in colors other than black. It is important for your own safety as well as for the safety of bears to learn how to hike and camp in bear country. The U.S. Forest Service and state wildlife agencies offer a great deal of information about these subjects.

Mountain lions have always been a secretive part of the dark forests in the Cabinets, but some people will go so far as to say there are more lions here for every 10 square miles than anywhere else in the nation. Within Sanders County, for instance, half of which lies within the Cabinets, mountain lions are thought to kill up to 15,000 deer each year.

Other predatory creatures living in the Cabinets include coyotes, bobcat, the threatened Canada lynx, wolverine, fisher and marten. And predatory birds such as bald eagles and golden eagles, osprey and a host of owls soar through the skies. Dozens of other birds, migratory and resident, reside in the Cabinets, too.

Terrestrial creatures are not alone in the Cabinet Mountains. Thousands of miles of streams and more than 200 lakes teem with all kinds of fishes, including native species that were here before man introduced a variety of others to the area's waters. Bull trout and westslope cutthroat trout were the only salmonids in the Cabinets a century ago. Now the former appears on the federal Endangered Species List and the latter may one day soon. In part, that is because other species have become well established and aggressively compete for food and space. Fishermen these days go for rainbow, brown and brook trout in many streams and lakes, while in warmer waters they find largemouth and smallmouth bass, yellow perch and northern pike.

Recreation

Though the Cabinets have undergone intense development over the past 120 years – from the time the railroads came through to the extraction of vast deposits of precious metals to the growing tourist industry – they remain a secluded, little-known range of mountains. Slowly that is changing. People from near and far are discovering the spectacular vistas, the well-maintained network of trails, the easy access, fine campgrounds, friendly communities and the opportunity for a rewarding rendezvous with nature.

From Bonners Ferry to Dixon, there are more than 180 trails meandering along almost 1,000 miles of terrain within the Cabinet Mountains. A lot of these trails are maintained on a regular basis and access remarkable destinations such as lakes, waterfalls, old-growth forests, forest fire lookout towers and stunning mountaintops. They are used by recreationists of all stripes – hunters, photographers, backpackers, picnickers, wildlife enthusiasts and anyone just wanting an experience of solitude in the backcountry.

People adventuring into the Cabinets get there in a variety of ways. Most people walk, many ride on horseback and a

Trish Gannon and her son, Dustin, arrive at Squaw Peak; Billiard Table Mountain is in the background.

growing cadre of hearty folk are riding mountain bikes. In winter, snowshoeing and cross-country skiing are growing in popularity. Motorized use with the likes of dirt bikes, ATVs and snowmobiles is also permissible on hundreds of miles of roads and even some trails. Remember, however, the wilderness is off-limits to both motorized vehicles and mountain bikes on all of its trails.

The Cabinets, for the most part, are not a pristine range of mountains. The settling of the valleys since the late 1800s has led to the development of this range's abundant natural resources, particularly timber. But there is a lot of wild country out there still at the disposal of all recreationists.

From Elmira Peak to Communion Butte; from Little Bitterroot Lake to Lake Pend Oreille; from the Thompson River to the Bull River to Boulder Creek, there is no shortage of hiking opportunities in the wild Cabinets, just a shortage of hikers. Hopefully, this guide will help direct you to some of the trails that best showcase the majesty of the land between the Clark's Fork of the Columbia and the Kootenai.

Nature programs are often presented at the historic Bull River Ranger Station.

Section I:

The Cabinet Mountains Wilderness

The Lay of the Land

The Cabinet Mountains Wilderness (CMW) was established by an act of Congress in 1964. It is about 35 miles long from north to south and is seldom more than 5 miles wide. At its widest, it stretches 7 miles between Crowell Creek and Mount Snowy (7,618 feet). Its narrowest section is in the West Fisher Creek drainage between Ojibway Peak (7,303 feet) and the Wayup Mine where the wilderness is less than a half-mile wide.

The northern and southern extremities of the CMW are marked by William Grambauer Mountain (7,377 feet) and Baree Mountain (6,050 feet on the map but actually over 6,400 feet). In between those two peaks are 25 others that surpass 7,000 feet. Although the elevations of the Cabinets' most prominent peaks are not very high relative to other mountain ranges in the Rockies, the vertical relief between valley floor and mountaintop is rather striking, nonetheless. In most cases there is well over 5,000 feet difference between the communities at the bottom of the mountains and the tops of the mountains themselves.

More than 100 lakes dot the subalpine country of the CMW. The majority of

Looking north from Engle Peak; notice Rock Lake in the right-center of photo.

the lakes have trails accessing them and harbor populations of feisty cutthroat trout. Wanless Lake in the south end is the largest, followed closely by Leigh Lake in the center of the wilderness on the west side of Snowshoe Peak. The highest lake is the uppermost Libby Lake, which nestles in a caldron of rock just shy of 7,000 feet. A short distance north is Isabella Lake at about 6,900 feet. Both lakes perch on opposite shoulders of Elephant Peak (7,938 feet).

The remnant of one alpine glacier still exists in the Cabinets. Blackwell Glacier resides on the north slope of Snowshoe Peak against the headwall of Granite Creek. A permanent snowfield sometimes referred to as Ibex Glacier can be found above Little Ibex Lake, and another vast snowfield sprawls across the headwaters of Ramsey Creek up against the cliffs of Elephant Peak. Tucked tightly into over-hanging rock at the headwaters of the West Fork of Blue Creek in the West Cabinets is another large snowfield that probably has not melted away entirely since the last Ice Age. Patches of snow sheltered by mountainous ramparts are often found in the high country throughout the summer.

Clean and pure are the simplest and most accurate terms to describe the water that comes out of the Cabinet Mountains Wilderness. Past studies have rated this water among the top 5 percent purest water in the Lower 48 states. Three and a half dozen streams tumble out of the high country, of which their waters end up either in the Clark Fork or Kootenai rivers. Both eventually flow into the Columbia.

A network of trails accesses the CMW from both sides. Libby, Montana, offers the primary jumping-off point on the east side while the west side – depending on where you want to go – can be accessed from Troy, Noxon or Trout Creek, Montana. More than 40 trails enter the wilderness. The north end enjoys a series of interconnected trails that provides convenient loop hikes. Trails into the central part of the wilderness are entirely in one way and back out the same way. The heart of the wilderness is simply too rugged to put trails through, though many avid hikers will often bushwhack over the Cabinet Divide, which is also the county line between Lincoln and Sanders counties in Montana. The south end also offers some loop hikes, though the best routes are open loops where it is more conven-ient to leave a vehicle at an exit trailhead.

The Cabinet Mountains Wilderness forms the heart of the Cabinet-Yaak Grizzly Bear Recovery Zone. Because grizzlies are on the federal Endangered Species List, a management plan has been devised with the aim of protecting adequate habitat throughout the grizzlies' present range in the Western United States. This is meant to help increase bear numbers so they have a chance for survival into the future. Though few grizzlies remain in the Cabinets, they are still there and from time to time people see them. Be cautious whenever hiking in bear country; take care of your food; and remember to always pack it in-pack it out.

A vast array of wildlife inhabits the wilderness and adjacent lands. Moose are common along stream bottoms, and mountain goats seem to cling impossibly to the narrowest ledges in many parts of the rocky high country. Encounters with wildlife are to be expected in the Cabinets, and it is always wisest to give wild ani-mals a wide berth.

The North End of the Cabinet Mountains Wilderness
William Grambauer Mountain to Flower Creek

Tucked tightly into a canyon between the Cabinet Mountains and the Purcell Mountains is a stretch of white water on the Kootenai River wild enough to have been chosen as the location for the filming of a Hollywood movie called "The River Wild" several years ago. The movie was okay; the scenery was fabulous.

From where the river gushes over fractured rock in a series of cascades known as Kootenai Falls, you can't quite see the summit of William Grambauer Mountain to the south, but it's up there, only two and a half miles away, and almost 5,400 feet above the churning rapids. Grambauer and its companion, Scenery Mountain, form the north boundary of the Cabinet Mountains Wilderness. Eight named peaks in this portion of the wilderness rise to more than 7,000 feet and no less than 18 lakes, small and large, are sheltered beneath their towering summits.

A well-connected series of trails accesses this area. Only two enter from the west side, and both of those trails are long, tough climbs, but three major trailheads on the east side provide for a variety of loop hikes. From Highway 56 and Highway 2 the north end of the CMW is a worthy destination for seasoned hikers.

William Grambauer Mountain at the north end of the CMW

Trails: William Grambauer, Scenery, Cedar Lakes, Taylor Peak, Dome, Minor Lake

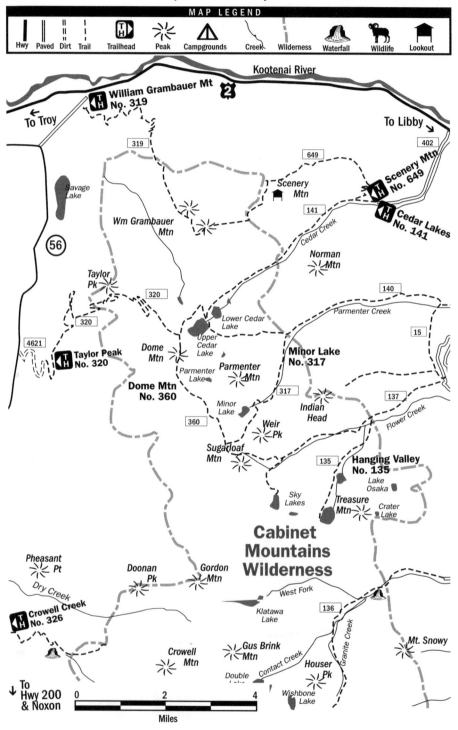

MAP LEGEND

| Hwy | Paved | Dirt | Trail | Trailhead | Peak | Campgrounds | Creek | Wilderness | Waterfall | Wildlife | Lookout |

Kootenai River

William Grambauer Mt
No. 319

To Troy →

To Libby →

319

649

402

Savage Lake

Scenery Mtn

Scenery Mtn
No. 649

141

Cedar Lakes
No. 141

56

Wm Grambauer Mtn

Cedar Creek

Norman Mtn

Taylor Pk

320

140

320

Lower Cedar Lake

Parmenter Creek

15

4621

Upper Cedar Lake

Taylor Peak
No. 320

Dome Mtn

Minor Lake
No. 317

Parmenter Lake

Parmenter Mtn

Dome Mtn
No. 360

317

137

Minor Lake

Indian Head

Flower Creek

360

Weir Pk

Sugarloaf Mtn

135

Hanging Valley
No. 135

Lake Osaka

Sky Lakes

Treasure Mtn

Crater Lake

Cabinet Mountains Wilderness

Pheasant Pt

Doonan Pk

Gordon Mtn

Dry Creek

West Fork

136

Klatawa Lake

Crowell Creek
No. 326

Mt. Snowy

Crowell Mtn

Gus Brink Mtn

Contact Creek

Houser Pk

Granite Creek

Double Lake

↓ To
Hwy 200
& Noxon

Wishbone Lake

0   2   4

Miles

William Grambauer Mountain Trail No. 319

Destination: William Grambauer Mountain, 7,377 feet. *Map, page 30.*

USGS Map: Kootenai Falls

Trailhead: About 4 miles southeast of Troy, Montana, on Highway 56 near mile-post 35, turn northeast onto a gravel road marked with a sign for the Old Highway 2 hiking trail. Go about a mile and a half to the parking area and the trailhead.

Trail Length: 7 miles one-way

Trail Condition: good

Elevation Gain: 4,900 feet

Estimated Duration of Hike: 5 to 6 hours up, 3 to 4 hours down

Sweat Index: strenuous

Best Features: great views of the Kootenai River Valley; traverses burned areas from forest fires in 1994 and 2000.

Availability of Water Along the Trail: virtually none

Stream Crossings: one small stream less than 2 miles from the trailhead

What's it like? William Grambauer was a prospector in the Bull River valley around the turn of the 20th century. Though not much information exists about the man now, he made enough of an impression in the old days to get a mountain and a stream named after him. William Grambauer Mountain marks the northernmost extent of the CMW and rises more than 5,300 vertical feet above the Kootenai River just 2.5 miles away. The trail begins on private property, though the Forest Service has an easement for the trailhead and the trail across private lands. A mile or so up Trail 319 are a series of rock ledges that offer some fine views of the Bull Lake and Kootenai valleys, Savage Lake and surrounding mountains. But once beyond those ledges, the trail enters a forest clinging to the steeply ascending mountainside and switchbacks time and time again on its relentless march to the top. Three thousand vertical feet later, the trail breaks over the lip of a ridge that provides some nice, level walking for a distance of nearly 2 miles. When you gain the ridgeline just south of the summit, you will be on the edge of a gigantic burn that consumed much of the northeast side of Cedar Creek in 1994. The top is a rocky knob affording expansive views from Troy to Libby and south along the spine of the wilderness.

Camping: not really

Precautions: An apparent trail junction not marked on any maps occurs on a switchback not far below the top. The old trail, no longer maintained, wends its way toward Upper Cedar Lake.

Alternate Hikes: Some maps indicate Trail No. 344, which is a maintained trail, going up William's Creek from Highway 2 and tying in with Trail 319 a mile or so north of the summit. From William Grambauer Mountain, Trail 319 continues east along the ridge to Scenery Mountain where it connects with Trail No. 649.

Scenery Mountain Trail No. 649

Destination: Scenery Mountain Lookout, 6,875 feet. *Map, page 30.*

USGS Map: Scenery Mountain

Trailhead: About 4 miles west of Libby, Montana, turn southwest off Highway 2 onto Cedar Creek Road No. 402; proceed 2.5 miles to the trailhead.

Trail Length: 5 miles one-way

Trail Condition: good

Elevation Gain: 4,200 feet

Scenery Mountain, showing the effects of the 1994 wildfire; notice the lookout tower, top right corner.

Estimated Duration of Hike: 3 to 4 hours up, 2 to 3 hours down

Sweat Index: strenuous

Best Features: terrific views of Cedar Creek, high peaks to the southwest and of Libby; a look at the effects of a large-scale forest fire; abandoned forest fire lookout tower. Wildlife, such as elk, utilizes this area a lot.

Availability of Water Along the Trail: none

Stream Crossings: none

What's it like? Trail 649 takes off from Cedar Creek Trail No. 141 about a mile from the trailhead, which includes a facility for loading and unloading horses. It climbs steeply to a ridgeline that ascends to the summit. Along the entire length of this trail, it either goes through or skirts the edge of a vast forest fire that burned here in 1994. Though a great deal of this landscape was blackened, many big old trees survived, and there are some dandy ponderosa pines scattered across the area. After the fire, the vistas that opened up of Cedar Creek and its surrounding peaks are breathtaking. The old lookout appears to be well used by pack rats, but a walk around its raised platform offers fabulous panoramas in all directions and leaves little question as to why this mountain was named Scenery.

Camping: There is no water anywhere close to the top of this mountain, but camping on the bald summit is a rewarding experience, especially at night when the lights of Libby come on and try to rival the lights in a clear, starry sky.

Precautions: Exposure in the summertime in areas intensely burned in 1994 can be brutally hot. Pack lots of water, wear sunglasses and use sunscreen.

Alternate Hikes: Trail 649 connects with Trail 319 at the lookout, which heads west to William Grambauer Mountain.

Cedar Lakes Trail No. 141

Destination: Cedar Lakes. *Map, page 30.*

USGS Map: Scenery Mountain

Trailhead: Four miles west of Libby, Montana, turn southwest off Highway 2 onto Cedar Creek Road No. 402 and proceed 2.5 miles to the trailhead.

Trail Length: 5 miles one-way

Trail Condition: excellent

Elevation Gain: 3,200 feet to the upper lake

Estimated Duration of Hike: 3 to 4 hours up, 2 to 3 hours down

Sweat Index: difficult

Best Features: high mountain lakes, fishing, old-growth forest

Availability of Water Along the Trail: This is a streamside trail most of the way to the lakes.

Stream Crossings: nothing significant

What's it like? Trail 141 follows relatively closely to Cedar Creek all the way to Lower Cedar Lake, which is accessed by a short spur trail. Old-growth forest lines the creek bottom, but flames from the 1994 Scenery Mountain Fire approached the creek in many places. The upper lake is about 400 vertical feet above the lower lake and sits in a basin walled with cliffs and crags rising to the unseen summit of Dome Mountain. Upper Cedar Lake is the third-largest lake in the CMW. Both have resident populations of cutthroat trout.

Lower Cedar Lake

Camping: Primitive campsites can be found at both lakes. To minimize impacts to the fragile wilderness environment, utilize existing campsites.

Alternate Hikes: Trail 141 is part of a network of trails that allows for open or closed loops in the north end of the wilderness. Consult a wilderness map to plan a variety of routes.

Taylor Peak Trail No. 320

Destination: Taylor Peak, Dome Mountain and Cedar Lakes. *Map, page 30.*

USGS Map: Crowell Mountain

Trailhead: Near milepost 30 on Highway 56 about 9 miles southeast of Troy, Montana, look for Taylor Peak Road No. 4621. Turn east onto that road and travel about a mile and a half to the trailhead. There's no parking right where the trail hits the road, so vehicles need to be left at the switchback below.

Trail Length: 8 miles one-way

Trail Conditions: good

Elevation Gain: 4,000 feet

Estimated Duration of Hike: 5 to 6 hours up, 4 to 5 hours down

Sweat Index: strenuous

Best Features: some wildlife viewing opportunities, gains access to the high country and ties in with other trails.

Availability of Water Along the Trail: One stream crossing about 2 miles up the trail may offer a trickle.

Stream Crossings: one minor crossing

What's it like? Trail 320 begins on state land, then climbs and climbs and climbs – and you think it will never stop climbing. But some interesting meadows dot the higher slopes and provide great views of the Bull Lake valley and the West Cabinets beyond. A short off-trail excursion will lead to the top of Taylor Peak at the headwaters of Falls Creek, which harbors a couple of small alpine lakes.

Camping: The lack of water makes camping along the Taylor Peak trail a little undesirable, but once on top of the Cabinet Divide there are wonderful opportunities for backcountry camping using Leave No Trace techniques. A small spring can be found north of Dome Mountain that can provide adequate water.

Alternate Hikes: Trail 320 ties in with Trail No. 360 and access to a network of trails in the north end of the CMW.

Looking south from Dome Mountain

Dome Mountain Trail No. 360

Destination: Dome Mountain, 7,560 feet. *Map, page 30.*

USGS Map: Crowell Mountain

Trailhead: Trail 360 is a connector trail for several trails accessing the wilderness. It ties together Cedar Creek Trail 141, page 33, and Flower Creek Trail 137, page 39, as well as Taylor Peak Trail 320, page 34.

Trail Length: 7 miles one-way

Trail Condition: good

Elevation Gain: 1,600 to 2,000 feet

Estimated Duration of Hike: 3 to 4 hours

Sweat Index: difficult

Best Features: high peaks, alpine basins, glacial lakes

Availability of Water Along the Trail: A small spring north of Dome Mountain offers adequate water.

Stream Crossings: none

What's it like? Spectacular is a great word to describe the country traversed by this trail. Putting in this trail was one of the best things done for hikers in the Cabinets, as it connects several high lakes and peaks in an alpine setting. This trail can be reached from Cedar Creek, Parmenter Creek, Flower Creek or Taylor Peak. At Upper Cedar Lake, Trail 360 begins its ascent to the summit of Dome Mountain, which is attained in about 3 miles and 1,600 feet. Expansive alpine meadows cloak these high ridges. From the other end, Trail 360 departs Trail 137 near Sky Lakes and enters a gap between Weir Peak and Sugarloaf Mountain. A small pothole lake resides here against a remarkable cliff falling straight off the 7,566-foot summit of Sugarloaf. An almost sheer wall nearly 900 feet high shades this section of the trail much of the year. In this gap another connecting trail descends to Minor Lake and hooks up with Parmenter Creek Trail 140 after about 4 miles. Four miles and 2,000 feet from Trail 137 is the top of Dome Mountain, which is characterized by a vast alpine meadow and scattered stunted trees.

Camping: Hikers can set up backcountry camps virtually anywhere along this trail, but because of the fragile high-elevation terrain, Leave No Trace ethics should be used.

Alternate Hikes: This trail connects Trails 141, 137, 317 and 320. It provides the opportunity for several loop hikes in the north end of the CMW. These loops, open or closed, can range from about 15 to 25 miles.

Minor Lake Trail No. 317

Destination: Minor Lake. *Map, page 30.*

USGS Map: Treasure Mountain

Trailhead: This is a connecting trail between Parmenter Trail 140, page 38, and Dome Mountain Trail 360, page 35.

Trail Length: 4 miles total; nearly 2.5 miles to the lake from Parmenter Trail 140

Trail Conditions: good

Elevation Gain: 1,200 feet to the lake from Parmenter Trail 140; 2,200 feet total elevation gain from Parmenter Trail 140 to Dome Mountain Trail 360.

Estimated Duration of Hike: 1 to 2 hours to the lake; 2 to 3 hours full length of trail

Sweat Index: difficult

Best Features: alpine lake, rugged peaks

Availability of Water Along the Trail: The South Fork Parmenter Creek flows parallel to the trail.

Stream Crossings: three minor crossings

What's it like? This trail accesses a beautiful lake nestled between Parmenter Mountain and Weir Peak. From the lake, it is a steep climb into a magical pass cradling a small unnamed pothole lake at the base of an incredible cliff falling straight off Sugarloaf Mountain.

Camping: Primitive campsites can be found at the lake.

Tim Nicholls snacks on a glacier lily.

Alternate Hikes: This is an important connecting trail between Parmenter Creek and Dome Mountain and allows for a variety of loop hikes in the north end of the wilderness.

Trails: Parmenter Creek, Flower Creek/Sky Lakes, Hanging Valley

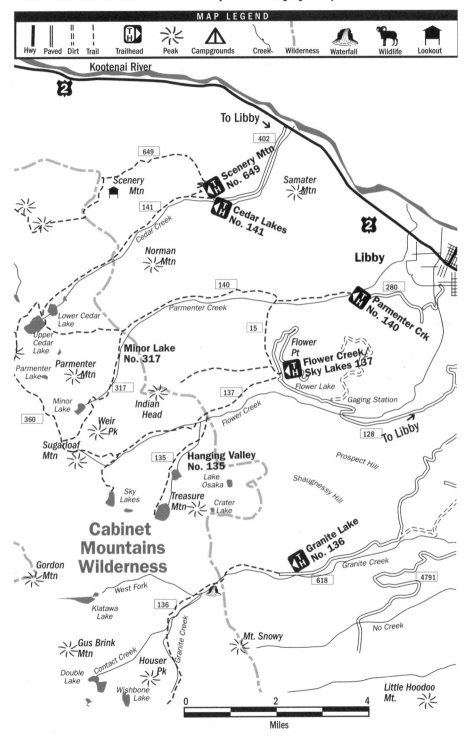

MAP LEGEND

| Hwy | Paved | Dirt | Trail | Trailhead | Peak | Campgrounds | Creek | Wilderness | Waterfall | Wildlife | Lookout |

Kootenai River

To Libby

402

649

Scenery Mtn No. 649

Scenery Mtn

Samater Mtn

141

Cedar Lakes No. 141

Cedar Creek

Norman Mtn

Libby

140

Parmenter Crk No. 140

280

Parmenter Creek

15

Lower Cedar Lake

Flower Pt

Upper Cedar Lake

Flower Creek Sky Lakes 137

Parmenter Lake

Minor Lake No. 317

Parmenter Mtn

Flower Lake

Gaging Station

317

Minor Lake

Indian Head

137

Flower Creek

360

Weir Pk

128 To Libby

Sugarloaf Mtn

135

Hanging Valley No. 135

Prospect Hill

Lake Osaka

Shaugnessy Hill

Sky Lakes

Treasure Mtn

Crater Lake

Cabinet Mountains Wilderness

Granite Lake No. 136

Gordon Mtn

Granite Creek

West Fork

618

4791

136

Klatawa Lake

Granite Creek

No Creek

Gus Brink Mtn

Contact Creek

Houser Pk

Mt. Snowy

Double Lake

Wishbone Lake

Little Hoodoo Mt.

0   2   4

Miles

Parmenter Creek Trail No. 140

Destination: Parmenter Creek, Upper Cedar Lake. *Map, page 37.*

USGS Map: Treasure Mountain

Trailhead: In Libby, Montana, at the intersection of Highways 2 and 37, turn west and go one block. Turn left on Main Street and, go 6 blocks to Balsam Street. Turn right, cross the Flower Creek Bridge, then take the first left and go 0.4 mile to the road that bears right up Parmenter Hill. At the top of the hill, take the first right and go just over a mile to the "Y." Take the unpaved left fork to the trailhead, about 200 yards.

Trail Length: 8.5 miles one-way

Trail Condition: excellent

Elevation Gain: 3,700 feet

Estimated Duration of Hike: 4 to 6 hours up, 4 to 5 hours down

Sweat Index: strenuous

Best Features: alpine lakes, rugged mountains

Availability of Water Along the Trail: Parmenter Creek parallels the trail much of the way.

Stream Crossings: Cross Parmenter Creek about a half-mile from the trailhead.

What's it like? For the most part this trail climbs at a gentle grade for the first 6 miles to the wilderness boundary and its junction with Trail 317. The stream is often nearby, filling the canyon with the music of flowing water. Trail 140 continues into the wilderness below the rugged spire of Parmenter Peak (7,345 feet) and switchbacks through a narrow notch called Parmenter Pass into the Cedar Lakes basin. A man-way, a primitive trail, about a mile and a half beyond the trail junction accesses two small lakes on the east side of Dome Mountain. The scenery is spectacular, and snow lingers long into the summer in the shadows of the surrounding high peaks.

Camping: Dispersed backcountry camping can be enjoyed at any of the lakes accessed from this trail. It is best to use existing campsites so as to minimize impacts to the lakeside environment.

Alternate Hikes: The Parmenter Creek Trail is part of a good loop hike with Flower Creek Trail 137 and Trails 15 and 317. An open loop is also doable between Parmenter and Cedar Creeks.

Flower Creek/Sky Lakes Trail No. 137

Destination: Flower Creek, Sky Lakes. *Map, page 37.*

USGS Map: Treasure Mountain

Trailhead: A half-mile south of Libby, Montana, turn west off Highway 2 onto Shaughnessy Hill Road. At the top of the hill go south a half-mile to Flower Creek Road No. 128 and turn west. Proceed 6 miles to the trailhead.

Trail Length: 6 miles one-way

Trail Condition: excellent

Elevation Gain: 3,700 feet

Estimated Duration of Hike: 3 to 4 hours up, 2 to 3 hours down

Sweat Index: difficult

Best Features: beautiful alpine lakes, rugged mountain scenery

Beargrass in full bloom

Availability of Water Along the Trail: The trail parallels Flower Creek much of the way.

Stream Crossings: nothing significant

What's it like? Flower Creek is a beautiful stream beginning in a couple of small lakes aptly named Sky Lakes. A broad basin opens up not far above the confluence of Hanging Valley Creek and gently rises to the base of triplet spires piercing the sky. Weir Peak (7,270 feet) is on the north, Sugarloaf Mountain (7,566 feet) dominates the center of the skyline and an unnamed peak rises to over 7,700 feet to the southwest. The rugged scenery is some of the best in the Cabinets. The trail ends at lower Sky Lake but it is a relatively easy climb to the smaller upper Sky Lake. On a bench above the northeast corner of the lake, amidst a stand of scattered alpine larch, is an Engelmann spruce that exceeds 5 feet in diameter and could well be one of the largest spruces in the wilderness. Alpine larch is abundant in this high basin and makes for a colorful spectacle in the autumn.

Camping: Good primitive camping opportunities exist at the lower lake.

Alternate Hikes: A mile and a half from lower Sky Lake, Trail 360 splits off from Trail 137 and ties in with Trail 317 to Minor Lake or goes to Dome Mountain and Cedar Lakes. A fabulous off-trail hike beginning at upper Sky Lake leads over the ridge between Sky Lakes and Hanging Valley, then follows Trail No. 135 back to Flower Creek. The Parmenter tie-in Trail No. 15 begins at the Flower Creek trailhead and connects with Parmenter Creek Trail No. 140 after about 2 miles.

Hanging Valley Trail No. 135

Destination: Hanging Valley. *Map, page 37.*

USGS Map: Treasure Mountain

Trailhead: Trail 135 is a spur trail off Flower Creek Trail 137, which is reached by going a half-mile south of Libby, Montana, and turning west off Highway 2 onto Shaughnessy Hill Road. At the top of the hill, go south a half-mile to Flower Creek Road No. 128 and turn west. Proceed 6 miles to the trailhead.

Trail Length: 3 miles one-way

Trail Condition: This is primarily a primitive trail, a "man-way," with steep grades, cliffs, downed trees and brush to contend with.

Elevation Gain: 2,000 feet

Estimated Duration of Hike: 2 to 3 hours up, 2 hours down

Sweat Index: strenuous

Best Features: A true, glacially sculpted valley is suspended high on the west flank of Treasure Mountain with a couple of large lakes. A thunderous, cascading waterfall leaves the lower lake, but it is tricky getting in position for a view.

Availability of Water Along the Trail: none until reaching the lower lake

Stream Crossings: none, except for crossing Flower Creek at the start

What's it like? Treasure Mountain forms a large part of the scenic backdrop to the town of Libby, but behind this backdrop is a scenic wonder called the Hanging Valley. Cradled in a basin between 5,800 and 6,400 feet, this glacial gem is a spectacular hidden treasure worth seeing. The summit of Treasure Mountain (7,694 feet) is attainable from here, and from that it is possible to reach several small lakes on the mountain's east face. But first you have to make it to Hanging Valley, and there is no easy way up. Trail 135 crosses Flower Creek from its junction with trail 137 and soon climbs tortuously straight up a rocky mountainside for more than 1,000 feet in barely a half-mile. Once over that, though, the basin – more than a square mile in size – begs to be explored.

Precautions: This is a rugged, steeply ascending trail not maintained for the average hiker.

Camping: Primitive camping can be enjoyed in Hanging Valley using Leave No Trace techniques. Not many people camp in this basin so impacts have been minor. By carefully selecting a suitable campsite, impacts can be minimized.

Alternate Hikes: Going off trail can make a cool loop hike from the upper lake over the ridge to the south and into Sky Lakes, then back down Trail 137.

The Central Part of Cabinet Mountains Wilderness
Granite Creek to Rock Lake

Millions of years ago, incredible pressure was exerted from deep beneath the earth's crust and pushed up the Cabinet Mountains. The pressure was greatest at the heart of the range and thrust a couple of spikes of sedimentary rock more than a thousand feet higher than most of the surrounding layers of ancient lake bed deposits. Those two "spikes" are known today as Snowshoe and A peaks and are the two highest mountains in the Cabinets at 8,736 feet and 8,634 feet, respectively.

Glaciers spent tens of thousands of years sculpting these high peaks and created a knife-edge divide that only the most experienced hikers can get over. That is why the trails of the central Cabinet Mountains Wilderness are pretty much all one way in and the same way back out. But the terrain and features accessed by these trails offer some of the most spectacular destinations in all of Montana.

Twenty-some lakes fill many of the glacial cirques in this part of the Cabinets, and virtually all of them offer fishing opportunities, though records indicate the only wilderness lake that had a native population of trout was Granite Lake. From Crowell Creek to Ozette Lake, the central CMW offers many of the most stunning hikes anywhere in the range.

One of several unnamed lakes in the Engle Lake Basin

Trails: Crowell Creek, North Fork Bull River, Middle Fork Bull River, Little Ibex Lake

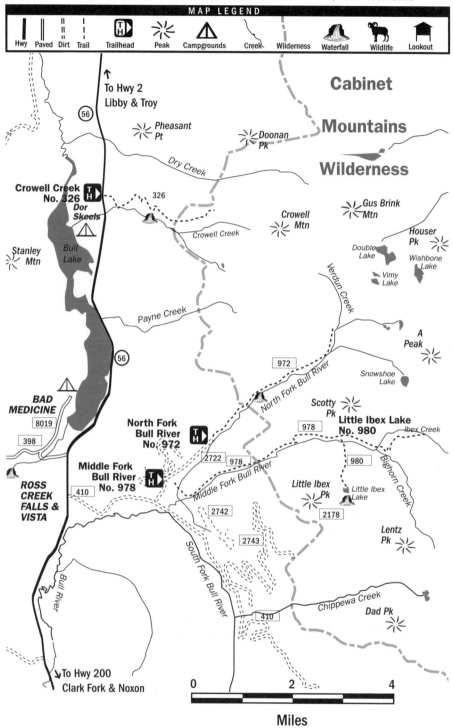

MAP LEGEND

| Hwy | Paved | Dirt | Trail | Trailhead | Peak | Campgrounds | Creek | Wilderness | Waterfall | Wildlife | Lookout |

To Hwy 2
Libby & Troy

56

Pheasant Pt

Doonan Pk

Dry Creek

Cabinet

Mountains

Wilderness

Crowell Creek
No. 326
Dor Skeels

326

Crowell Creek

Crowell Mtn

Gus Brink Mtn

Houser Pk

Double Lake

Wishbone Lake

Stanley Mtn

Bull Lake

Vimy Lake

Verdun Creek

Payne Creek

56

972

North Fork Bull River

A Peak

Snowshoe Lake

BAD MEDICINE
8019

398

North Fork
Bull River
No. 972

2722   978

978

Scotty Pk

Little Ibex Lake
No. 980

Ibex Creek

ROSS CREEK FALLS & VISTA

Middle Fork
Bull River
No. 978

410

Middle Fork Bull River

2742

2743

980

Little Ibex Pk

Little Ibex Lake

2178

Bighorn Creek

Lentz Pk

South Fork Bull River

Bull River

410

Chippewa Creek

Dad Pk

To Hwy 200
Clark Fork & Noxon

0   2   4

Miles

Crowell Creek Trail No. 326

Destination: Crowell Creek. *Map, page 42.*

USGS Map: Crowell Mountain

Trailhead: Near milepost 22 on Montana Highway 56 look for the small Forest Service trail sign on the east side of the highway. This obscure trailhead is about 16 miles south of Troy, Montana. The trail begins on private property and continues for more than a mile on state lands. Though the Forest Service does not have an easement on the private property next to the highway, the present landowner is agreeable to public use of the trail. Hikers should exercise the utmost respect for private property when passing through. This trailhead may be relocated within the next few years.

Trail Length: 3 miles one-way

Crowell Creek Falls

Trail Condition: This trail first follows a narrow road for a couple of hundred yards that accesses a domestic water supply. The trail veers north from the road (look for a rock cairn) before reaching the creek and climbs above private property onto state land. The tread is in good shape.

Elevation Gain: 3,000 feet

Estimated Duration of Hike: 1 to 2 hours up, less than 2 hours down

Sweat Index: moderate

Best Features: waterfall

Availability of Water Along the Trail: A few small trickles cross the trail higher up.

Stream Crossings: none

What's it like? About a mile from the highway a spur trail descends steeply into a narrow canyon to the base of a nice waterfall that is in three tiers and totals more than 100 feet. Beyond that the trail climbs steadily through a young forest of larch and lodgepole pine and enters the wilderness about two miles in. Another mile farther it dissipates into a slope of talus rock. Views of Bull Lake and Bad Medicine cliffs can be snatched through the trees from time to time.

Camping: no suitable campsites readily available

Precautions: Extreme caution should be exercised near the waterfall; rocks and logs are slippery and the slope is very steep.

Alternate Hikes: Off-trail hikers can continue beyond the end of the trail to Crowell Mountain (7,000-plus feet) and Gus Brink Mountain (7,041 feet) and some fine, ridge-top hiking.

North Fork Bull River Trail No. 972

Destination: Snowshoe Lake. *Map, page 42.*

USGS Map: Ibex Peak, Snowshoe Peak

Trailhead: About 20 miles north of Noxon, Montana turn east onto the South Fork Bull River Road No. 410 at milepost 16 on Highway 56. About two miles off the highway, the road forks – bear right and travel another mile to Road No. 2722 and turn northeast, then proceed about 2 miles to the trailhead.

Trail Length: 3 miles of trail, 2-plus miles of man-way

Trail Condition: A well-maintained trail exists to Verdun Creek where the trail forks into a pair of "man-ways," a non-maintained trail. One goes to Snowshoe Lake and the other ascends Verdun Creek toward Vimy Ridge. A small sign nailed to a spruce tree marks the end of the maintained trail. The final stretch of the trail to Snowshoe Lake includes a difficult scramble up an imposing cliff face just below the lake.

Elevation Gain: 3,200 feet to the lake

Estimated Duration of Hike: 4 to 5 hours up, 3 to 4 hours down

Sweat Index: strenuous

Best Features: alpine lake, waterfalls, rugged peaks

Availability of Water Along the Trail: The trail closely follows the North Fork Bull River much of the way.

Stream Crossings: minor crossing at Verdun Creek and the crisscrossing of small streams on the way to the lake.

What's it like? Trail 972 begins innocently enough alongside a merry stream in a forested valley. A couple of miles along the trail, an open expanse of flat rocks flank the North Fork Bull River and a pleasant waterfall. Once past Verdun Creek, where the trail forks into man-ways, the going gets tougher heading toward Snowshoe Lake until the hiker is faced with a wall of rock that seems to preclude reaching the lake. It is a scramble to get up it, but the climb is doable and the rewards are great. Snowshoe Lake glistens in a magnificent cirque of meadows and rock fields flanked by A Peak to the northeast and Snowshoe Peak to the southeast. The 2,600-foot rise to Snowshoe's lofty summit is daunting, but many hikers have conquered the ascent and marveled at the view of the Cabinets and beyond from the highest peak in the range.

Camping: Primitive campsites can be found near the lake and some fine back-country camping opportunities abound in Verdun Creek below Crowell Mountain.

Alternate Hikes: Snowshoe Lake is a traditional beginning point for a climb to the top of Snowshoe Peak. This is not a technical climb, but there is exposure along the way on steep, loose rock. Most people will stay a night at the lake, summit the peak the following day and return to the lake for one more night before hiking out.

Middle Fork Bull River Trail No. 978
and Little Ibex Lake Trail No. 980

Destination: Middle Fork Bull River, Little Ibex Lake, and Ibex Creek. *Map, page 42.*

USGS Map: Ibex Peak

Trailhead: About 20 miles north of Noxon, Montana turn east onto the South Fork Bull River Road No. 410 at milepost 16 on Highway 56. About two miles off the highway the road forks – bear right and travel another mile to Road No. 2722 and turn northeast. Turn right after about 1 mile onto a narrow dirt road and go 100 yards to the trailhead.

Trail Length: No. 978 dead-ends after about 6 miles; follow trail No. 978 nearly 4 miles to its obscure junction with trail No. 980 marked by a rock cairn, and look for blazes below the main trail; No. 980 is about 2 miles to the lake and climbs very steeply for the last half-mile.

Trail Conditions: Trail No. 978 is well-maintained by the Forest Service, though during high water, a section about 2 miles in is under water; Trail No. 980 to the lake is no longer maintained by the Forest Service and is degenerating into a man-way. Expect lots of blowdown across the trail, fading blazes and sometimes obscure tread.

Elevation Gain: 2,700 feet to Little Ibex Lake

Estimated Duration of Hike: 3 to 4 hours to Little Ibex Lake or to Ibex Creek Meadows, 2.5 to 3.5 hours down

Sweat Index: strenuous

Best Features: alpine lake, waterfall, spectacular rugged mountain views, glacier remnants, wildlife

Availability of Water Along the Trail: Trail No. 978 closely follows the Middle Fork Bull River; lots of springs feed the lake.

Stream Crossings: three major crossings on narrow logs and one wading

A view from Middle Fork Bull River Trail

What's it like? The primary destination on the Middle Fork Bull River Trail is Little Ibex Lake. It's in a gorgeous basin that catches meltwater from the abundant snow that accumulates on the east side of Ibex Peak. It has no fish. But the pristine alpine setting is as spectacular as any wilderness lake anywhere. From the lake's west shore you get a fantastic view of the highest peak in the Cabinets – Snowshoe – and if you climb among the rocks above the lake, the view just gets better. The scenery is dramatic, the water in the lake is cold and refreshing, and you just might get a glimpse of some mountain goats. A nice waterfall 15 to 20 feet high spills from the stream flowing into the lake at its south end. The hike along the Middle Fork Bull River is a pleasant, relatively easy stroll, often near enough to the stream to enjoy the cooling effects of its strong perennial flow. In season keep an eye out for the Rocky Mountains' only single-flowered wintergreen, the wood nymph. Views of Little Ibex Peak unfold above the narrow valley as you proceed up the trail. Beyond its junction with Little Ibex Lake Trail, No. 978 becomes less hospitable until it finally peters out deep into the basin below Snowshoe Peak. But there are some beautiful meadows and a couple of tiny pothole lakes to enjoy deep in this part of the wilderness.

Camping: Primitive backcountry camping can be enjoyed near the lake and in the vast meadows in Ibex and Bighorn creeks.

Alternate Hikes: Trail No. 978 ends in Ibex Creek but offers access to fabulous cross-country hiking in the high basin south of Snowshoe Peak. A couple of small, unnamed lakes are located there. The trail will climb steeply alongside a magnificent cascading waterfall for several hundred vertical feet. Adventurous explorers might want to climb through the rugged terrain up to the remnants of Ibex Glacier south of the lake and explore the permanent snowfields clinging to the protected north slope of the ridge.

Little Ibex Lake

Trails: Granite Creek, Leigh Lake

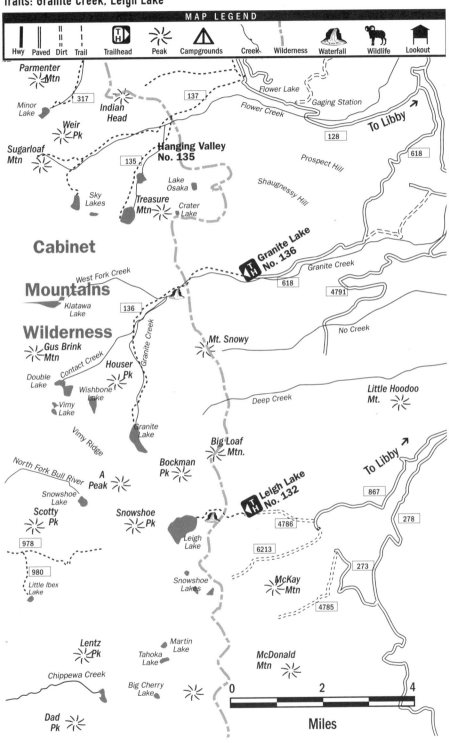

MAP LEGEND

| Hwy | Paved | Dirt | Trail | Trailhead | Peak | Campgrounds | Creek | Wilderness | Waterfall | Wildlife | Lookout |

Parmenter Mtn

Minor Lake

317

Indian Head

Weir Pk

Sugarloaf Mtn

Flower Lake

137

Flower Creek

Gaging Station

To Libby

128

135

Hanging Valley No. 135

Prospect Hill

618

Lake Osaka

Sky Lakes

Treasure Mtn

Crater Lake

Shaugnessy Hill

Cabinet

West Fork Creek

Granite Lake No. 136

Granite Creek

Mountains

Klatawa Lake

136

618

4791

Wilderness

Gus Brink Mtn

Contact Creek

Houser Pk

Granite Creek

Mt. Snowy

No Creek

Double Lake

Wishbone Lake

Vimy Lake

Vimy Ridge

Granite Lake

Deep Creek

Little Hoodoo Mt.

Big Loaf Mtn.

Bockman Pk

North Fork Bull River

A Peak

Snowshoe Lake

Scotty Pk

978

980

Little Ibex Lake

Snowshoe Pk

Leigh Lake

Snowshoe Lakes

Leigh Lake No. 132

To Libby

867

278

4786

6213

273

McKay Mtn

4785

Lentz Pk

Tahoka Lake

Martin Lake

McDonald Mtn

Chippewa Creek

Big Cherry Lake

Dad Pk

0   2   4

Miles

Granite Creek Trail No. 136

Destination: Granite Lake. *Map, page 47.*

USGS Map: Treasure Mountain, Snowshoe Peak

Trailhead: A half mile south of Libby, Montana, turn west off Highway 2 onto Shaughnessy Hill Road; at the top of the hill go south almost a half mile to a sharp, easy-to-miss turn west onto Flower Creek Road 128. A mile along that, turn east onto Forest Road No. 618 and follow it 8 miles to the trailhead. The last 2 miles are narrow and rocky, and there are several spur roads leading into the Lukens-Hazel Mine.

Granite Creek with A Peak in background and Snowshoe Peak, far left

Trail Length: 6 miles one-way

Trail Condition: good

Elevation Gain: 1,400 feet

Estimated Duration of Hike: 4 to 5 hours up, 3 to 4 hours down

Sweat Index: strenuous

Best Features: waterfalls, spectacular cliffs, view of Blackwell Glacier, wildlife

Availability of Water Along the Trail: plenty of water

Stream Crossings: four stream crossings, several with logs

What's it like? Granite Creek is a steep-walled, narrow valley with a classic, glacial U-shape. No wonder, as the only remaining alpine glacier in the Cabinets clings to the headwall of the drainage on Snowshoe Peak. Though the trail accesses only Granite Lake, four other magnificent alpine lakes are located in tributary creeks. Klatawa Lake is 1,600 feet up the West Fork of Granite Creek; Double Lake, Vimy Lake and Wishbone Lake are all in Contact Creek between 1,400 and 2,000 feet above the main Granite Creek valley. They are all accessible if you're interested in some difficult off-trail hiking along barely discernible "man-ways." About 2 miles along the trail, not far inside the wilderness boundary, is a beautiful 10-foot-high waterfall and a deep, emerald-blue plunge pool. At the head end of Granite Lake, one of the most dramatic cascading waterfalls anywhere in the Rockies carves a notch for nearly a thousand vertical feet. This stream flows directly from Blackwell Glacier. Two of the largest Douglas fir trees in Montana can be seen along the trail. The first is only a mile and a half from the trailhead and is more than 5 feet in diameter and perhaps 150 feet tall. The other is less than 2 miles from the lake on the edge of an avalanche chute in a grove of giant trees. Though not as tall as the first one, it appears to be thicker with a trunk that may exceed 6 feet in diameter. Though the summit of Snowshoe Peak is visible from the north end of the lake, the looming buttress of A Peak is the grandest spectacle along this trail. It becomes a dominant feature while still over 2 miles away, but once at the lake, its spectacularly rugged head rises more than 4,000 vertical feet above the lake's shimmering surface.

Camping: Primitive campsites exist near the lake.

Precautions: This valley seems to be a favorite haunt for moose, which have poor eyesight, are long-legged and don't care where they step. The stream crossings can be tricky during high water, so beware of slick logs!

Alternate Hikes: Off-trail hiking from the lake to the glacier is possible, but expect the route to be extremely difficult.

Leigh Lake Trail No. 132

Destination: Leigh Lake. *Map, page 47.*

USGS Map: Snowshoe Peak

Trailhead: Approximately 8 miles south of Libby, Montana, turn west off Highway 2 onto Big Cherry Creek Road No. 278. After 3 miles turn west again onto Road No. 867 and proceed 5 miles to the junction of Road No. 4786 and follow it about 2 miles to the trailhead.

Leigh Lake with Snowshoe Peak in the far background

Trail Length: 1.5 miles one-way

Trail Condition: Mostly in good shape, the trail's final half-mile, however, is steep and rocky. The trail forks at the bottom of a waterfall, and the better trail crosses the stream and climbs up through brush and cliffs. The right fork switchbacks through rock outcrops and becomes braided and easy to lose in the brush. Arrows have been painted on some rocks to indicate the direction to go, but the difficult climb still makes finding the trail a little confusing.

Elevation Gain: 900 feet

Estimated Duration of Hike: 1 to 2 hours up, 1 to 2 hours down

Sweat Index: moderate

Best Features: spectacular alpine lake, waterfall, rugged peaks

Availability of Water Along the Trail: Good water can be found at the falls where the trail forks about a mile from the trailhead.

Stream Crossings: one relatively easy crossing if you take the south fork

What's it like? The hike to Leigh Lake is pretty short but quite steep; especially for a short scramble perhaps 200 to 300 feet up over the lip of the basin cradling the lake. Once above this impasse, the cirque in which this, the second largest lake in the wilderness, resides is stunningly beautiful. Snowshoe Peak rises 3,600 feet to the west, and Bockman Peak stands guard to the north. An excursion onto the ridge southeast of the lake really brings the entire setting into an unparalleled view of the rugged grandeur of this alpine valley. A partial view of Blackwell Glacier can be obtained from this ridge. A wonderful picnic site is located on the north shore of the lake. One of Montana's largest-known grand firs is located along the trail. Its trunk exceeds 4 feet in diameter.

Camping: This lake is a popular destination because the hike is so short, which means campers have compacted numerous areas near the lake. Several good campsites are at the southeast edge of the lake, but exercise extreme care so as not to adversely impact this sensitive habitat any further.

Alternate Hikes: There is opportunity for some good off-trail hiking on the ridge and slopes south of the lake. Many people use this as the place to launch an assault on Snowshoe Peak's high summit.

Trails: Dad Peak, St. Paul Lake, Moran Basin, Rock Lake, Cliff Lake

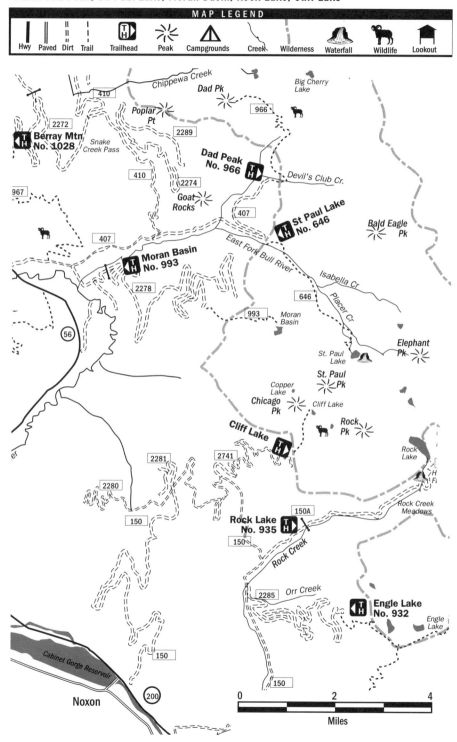

MAP LEGEND

| Hwy | Paved | Dirt | Trail | Trailhead | Peak | Campgrounds | Creek | Wilderness | Waterfall | Wildlife | Lookout |

Chippewa Creek

Big Cherry Lake

Dad Pk

410

Poplar Pt

966

2272

2289

Berray Mtn No. 1028

Snake Creek Pass

Dad Peak No. 966

Devil's Club Cr.

410

2274

Goat Rocks

967

St Paul Lake No. 646

Bald Eagle Pk

407

407

East Fork Bull River

Isabella Cr

Moran Basin No. 993

2278

646

Placer Cr

56

993

Moran Basin

Elephant Pk

St. Paul Lake

St. Paul Pk

Copper Lake

Chicago Pk

Cliff Lake

Rock Pk

Cliff Lake

Rock Lake

2281

2741

Rock Lake

2280

150

150A

Rock Lake No. 935

Rock Creek Meadows

150

150

Rock Creek

2285

Orr Creek

Engle Lake No. 932

Engle Lake

Cabinet Gorge Reservoir

150

Noxon

200

150

0   2   4
Miles

Dad Peak Trail No. 966

Destination: Dad Peak, Lentz Peak. *Map, page 51.*

USGS Map: Snowshoe Peak

Trailhead: About 13 miles north of Noxon, Montana, turn east off Highway 56 at milepost 8 and proceed on Road No. 407 about 8 miles to the trailhead.

Trail Length: 6 miles one-way

Trail Condition: The Forest Service is not presently maintaining this trail, but other trail users are. The tread becomes a bit obscure where it crosses the higher meadows, but all in all, this trail is in fair to good shape.

Elevation Gain: 3,000 feet

Estimated Duration of Hike: 4 to 5 hours up, 3 to 4 hours down

Sweat Index: strenuous

Best Features: rugged peaks, alpine meadows, wildlife

Availability of Water Along the Trail: Water can be taken from Devil's Club Creek and from the North Fork of the East Fork Bull River.

Stream Crossings: The first crossing has a log that can be a little tricky; the second crossing is difficult and requires extreme caution.

What's it like? It is possible this trail encounters a greater variety of habitats than any other trail in the CMW. An old-growth forest dominates the first mile or so and includes ancient cedars, hemlocks, whitepine and other tree species. A luxuriant array of plant life carpets the forest floor. Once across Devil's Club Creek, the trail joins an old road that once provided access to areas that were clear-cut back in the 1960s. The road is overgrown now and maintained as a trail. Beyond the old clear-cut, the trail enters the wilderness and a remarkable stand of timber that was burned in 1994. Thousands of acres were charred then, and much of it was old-growth cedar. The giant snags left behind are testimony to the ferocity of the fire. Higher up the mountainside, the trail traverses vast open meadows before reaching the ridgeline and the site where a forest fire lookout tower once stood on Dad Peak. Elk and mule deer are plentiful in this basin, and bighorn sheep can often be seen on a cliffy mountainside called the Goat Rocks.

Camping: Ridgeline camping is available at the end of this trail, and some people use this route for access to Chippewa Lake for overnight campouts.

Alternate Hikes: This trail accesses a high ridge that provides some superb off-trail hiking to Lentz Peak and Alaska Peak and good views of Chippewa Lake.

St. Paul Lake Trail No. 646

Destination: St. Paul Lake. *Map, page 51.*

USGS Map: Elephant Peak

Trailhead: Turn east off Highway 56 at milepost 8 about 13 miles north of Noxon, Montana, and proceed 6 miles on Road No. 407 to the trailhead.

Trail Length: 4 miles one-way

Trail Condition: excellent

Elevation Gain: 1,600 feet

Estimated Duration of Hike: 2 to 3 hours up, 1.5 to 2.5 hours down

Sweat Index: difficult

St. Paul Lake

Best Features: old-growth forest, alpine lake, rugged peaks

Availability of Water Along the Trail: Several streams provide good water along the way.

Stream Crossings: three crossings starting with the one at Isabella Creek that has a log to cross on, as does the third crossing. The second stream crossing at Placer Creek has a footbridge.

What's it like? Hiking on a hot summer's day could not be nicer than along this shady trail through the old-growth forest of the East Fork Bull River. Giant cedars and hemlocks intertwine their branches high overhead for practically the entire length of this trail. The nearby stream harbors feisty little cutthroat trout; look along its edges for the rare Northern beech fern. An interesting spring is located next to the trail about 2 miles up from the trailhead. The water is crystal clear, and the bubbling sand indicates where it seeps from below ground. Look carefully and you just might spy a shy frog hiding in its silty bottom. Don't disturb! Farther along, just beyond the Placer Creek crossing, a giant Western white pine stands like a sentinel along the trail at a switchback. Though many of its kindred have succumbed to the blister rust disease, this tree, some 4 to 5 feet in diameter – is still alive and seemingly in good health. The lake is nearly a perfect circular pothole with an extremely brushy shoreline, which makes access a bit difficult. Slabs of sedimentary rock protruding from St. Paul Peak south of the lake are laced with small waterfalls and make for some interesting exploration.

Camping: Primitive campsites can be found near the lake's north edge, but adventurous hikers may want to explore the ledges south of the lake and camp up above its glimmering waters.

Alternate Hikes: Off-trail hikers like to continue south of St. Paul Lake over St. Paul Pass to Rock Lake. It is a fabulous cross-country open loop hike that can be done in a day but is best enjoyed overnight.

Moran Basin Trail No. 993

Destination: Moran Basin. *Map, page 51.*

USGS Map: Elephant Peak

Trailhead: About 13 miles north of Noxon, Montana, at milepost 8 on Highway 56, turn east onto Road No. 407 and go 1.5 miles to Road 2278. Follow it less than 1 mile to the Historic Bull River Ranger Station. Just past the station, continue on the main road by turning east and follow it one-quarter mile to a permanently closed gate.

Trail Length: 13 miles one-way

Trail Condition: The first 6 miles of this trail is actually a road that is occasionally used by the Forest Service and its contractors. The next 5 miles are still on the road, but it becomes more overgrown and is maintained as a trail. The final 2 miles into the lake are along a real trail.

Elevation Gain: 3,800 feet

Estimated Duration of Hike: By foot this hike will take 6 to 8 hours up, but a mountain bike can make the first 11 miles go by in an hour or so. The 2 miles of trail can be hiked in an hour or so each way. A mountain bike stashed near the end of the road can make for about a 30-minute ride back to the gate.

Sweat Index: difficult

Best Features: alpine lake, wildlife

Availability of Water Along the Trail: There is usually at least a trickle of water in a couple of streams along the road.

Stream Crossings: Gated Road 2278 crosses two streams.

What's it like? Lost Girl Road No. 2278 is a terrific mountain biking path, but once at the end of the road, leave the bike. You enter the wilderness here and bikes aren't allowed. It is okay, though, as the trail is a relatively easy jaunt to the ridgeline, and then a steep descent takes you into the lake basin. While walking, pedaling or horseback riding up the road, the views of the Bull River Valley and the West Cabinets are excellent. Once on the ridge, the views switch to the wilderness, and Bald Eagle Peak, Elephant Peak and St. Paul Peak are breathtaking. Moran Lake harbors lots of hungry trout for such a small lake.

Camping: Several primitive campsites can be found at the lake.

Precautions: This area was the site of several grizzly bear releases during the 1990s, and it is known as a favorite haunt for both kinds of bears – blacks and grizzlies. Other wildlife is plentiful here, too, such as moose and elk.

Alternate Hikes: Another popular way to access Moran Basin is to hike off trail across the western flank of St. Paul Peak from the end of the Chicago Peak Road.

Rock Lake Trail No. 935

Destination: Rock Lake. *Map, page 51.*

USGS Map: Elephant Peak

Trailhead: Two miles east of Noxon, Montana, turn north off Highway 200 near milepost 17 onto Rock Creek Road No. 150. After a couple hundred yards take the right fork and go about 6 miles to the junction of Road No. 150A and take it 1.5 miles to the trailhead.

Trail Length: 4 miles one-way

Trail Condition: The first 2.5 miles are along an old mining road, and thence on a well-maintained trail to the lake.

Rock Lake

Elevation Gain: 2,800 feet

Estimated Duration of Hike: 2 to 3 hours up, 1 to 2 hours down

Sweat Index: difficult

Best Features: historic mining activity, alpine lake, fishing, waterfall, wildlife (moose, grizzly bears)

Availability of Water Along the Trail: Several streams cross the trail.

Stream Crossings: Within a couple hundred yards of the trailhead is the most difficult stream crossing. Early in the season the water flow is high and makes it nearly impossible to get across. As the summer wears on, the flow subsides.

What's it like? Road No. 150A is an old mining road that accessed the Heidelberg Mine in its heyday. A great deal of mining debris remains near Rock Creek Meadows, including two dilapidated cabins. Concrete and steel mill works can still be viewed below the falls at the end of the old road. A fantastic waterfall can be viewed southeast of the meadows in the direction of Lost Horse Mountain (7,508 feet). The meadows were the site of a beaver farm in the middle 1900s, and it is not unusual to see moose feeding among the marshy grasses and shrubs. The trail takes off from the road at the falls by the old mine works and switchbacks nearly 800 feet in elevation to the lake. The higher up the trail the more spectacular the view of the meadows and the Rock Creek drainage. Towering above the lake's outlet is the nearly vertical, gigantic rock slab of Ojibway Peak (7,303 feet).

Camping: This is a popular site with overnight hikers. Several primitive campsites can be found at the south end of the lake.

Precautions: Grizzly bears are known to utilize this area; two old mining cabins still stand along the trail at Rock Creek Meadows, but they are in an advanced stage of deterioration and should be avoided; the site of the Heidelberg Mine still allows access to an open shaft, but entrance into the tunnel is strongly advised against. Another shaft can be found above Rock Lake's outlet but it, too, should be left alone.

Trail to Cliff Lake (no designated trail number)

Destination: Chicago Peak, 7,006 feet, St. Paul Peak, 7,714 feet, and Cliff Lake. *Map, page 51.*

USGS Map: Elephant Peak

Trailhead: Two miles east of Noxon, Montana, near milepost 17, turn north off Highway 200 onto Rock Creek Road No. 150. After a couple hundred yards take the right fork and follow the road nearly 8 miles to Chicago Peak Road No. 2741. This road climbs some 2,600 feet to the unofficial trailhead and is narrow, strewn with rocks and crosses several deep gullies. Four-wheel-drive, high-clearance vehicles are recommended, and on the last 3 miles they are required. This is a rough road and it takes longer to drive to the trailhead than it does to hike to the lake.

Trail Length: 1.5 miles one-way

Trail Condition: Though there is a registration box at this trailhead, the Forest Service explains this is not actually an official trail, so it doesn't have a number and receives only minimal maintenance. Nonetheless, the path is in good shape.

Elevation Gain: 300 feet to Cliff Lake

Estimated Duration of Hike: 1 hour in, 1 hour out

Sweat Index: easy

Best Features: alpine lake, spectacular peaks, wildlife (mountain goats)

Availability of Water Along the Trail: Snow lingers late into the summer in Milwaukee Pass and collects in small pools throughout this alpine setting. Several small brooks usually have running water year-round.

Stream Crossings: There are numerous sensitive marshy areas and small brooks that should be avoided.

What's it like? The vehicle journey to this trail is much more difficult than the hike itself. But once there, nowhere in the wilderness is as easy to get to, nor as spectacular. A slight climb for a quarter-mile gains a magnificent viewpoint overlooking Milwaukee Pass and high, jagged peaks seemingly at arm's length. The trail then descends gently into the alpine meadows at the base of the fortress-like walls of Chicago Peak. This is a fragile environment that requires the utmost care of every hiker. Stay on the path or on the rocks at all times! The vegetation here is delicate and fragile. The trail meanders to a gorgeous view of Copper Lake before stepping down a stony face to the shoreline of Cliff Lake. Mountain goats often wander throughout this area. The more adventurous hiker might want to tackle the climb to St. Paul Peak (7,714 feet) from here for awesome views in every direction.

Camping: Primitive campsites are located near Cliff Lake.

Alternate Hikes: This access provides popular off-trail routes to the tops of St. Paul Peak, Chicago Peak and Rock Peak.

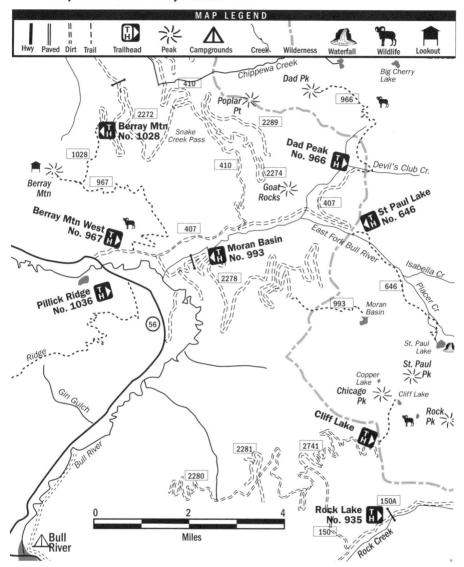

MAP LEGEND

| Hwy | Paved | Dirt | Trail | Trailhead | Peak | Campgrounds | Creek | Wilderness | Waterfall | Wildlife | Lookout |

Berray Mountain Trail West No. 967 and Berray Mountain Trail No. 1028

Destination: Berray Mountain Lookout, 6,177 feet

USGS Map: Ibex Peak

Trailhead: For No. 967, turn east off Highway 56 at milepost 8 about 13 miles north of Noxon, Montana, and go about 1 mile on Road No. 407 to the trailhead; for No. 1028, turn east off Highway 56 at the 16-mile marker about 20 miles north of Noxon and follow the South Fork Bull River Road No. 410 about 6 miles to the junction of Road No. 2272. Take that road 7 miles to the trailhead. The last couple miles of this road are narrow and steep with tight switchbacks.

Trail Length: 5 miles one-way on No. 967; 2.5 miles one-way to the lookout on No. 1028 and Trail 967.

Trail Conditions: good

Elevation Gain: 3,800 feet on No. 967; 700 feet on No. 1028

Estimated Duration of Hike: For No. 967, 3 to 4 hours up, 2 to 3 hours down; for No. 1028, 2 to 3 hours up, 1 to 2 hours down

Sweat Index: strenuous for No. 967; moderate for No. 1028

Best Features: great views of the Cabinet Mountains Wilderness and the West Cabinets, old forest fire lookout tower

Availability of Water Along the Trails: none

Stream Crossings: none

What's it like? The top of Berray Mountain can be accessed from either the East Fork Bull River on Trail No. 967 or from the South Fork Bull River on Trail

No. 1028. Berray Mountain is not actually part of the CMW, but it forms an important habitat link between the wilderness and the West Cabinets. Either trail is well worth the hike. No. 967 climbs through an open forest of pines and firs onto a gently ascending ridge and provides great views of Berray Mountain's south flank, where it is not unusual to see elk and mule deer. The two trails converge about a mile or so from the top of the mountain where an old Forest Service forest fire lookout tower is situated. An effort is under way to preserve the historic structure. The 360-degree view from the summit is incomparable with rugged peaks and ridges encircling this "island peak" in the heart of the Bull River valley.

Camping: Remember there is no water along these trails, but camping on top of Berray Mountain is a wonderful experience.

Berray Mountain Lookout

The South End of the Cabinet Mountains Wilderness
Engle Lake to Baree Lake

The centerpiece of the Cabinet Mountains Wilderness' south end is its largest lake, Wanless. A tea-spout waterfall plunges from the lake into a small pool full of cut-throat trout. Then the stream tumbles and churns down a rocky facade to the lush meadows around Buck Lake and thence for another 15 miles south and west as Swamp Creek to the Clark Fork River.

The south end is the smallest section of the wilderness, but it has some of the finest country to explore. Flattop Mountain, Engle Peak and Carney Peak are the only 7,000-plus-footers, but the Cabinet Divide and the upper portions of the East Fork of Rock Creek and Swamp Creek harbor many hidden areas of wild, rugged cliffs and basins.

A good system of interconnected trails provides for numerous, open-loop hikes accessing the string of small lakes on the east side of the divide as well as the Wanless Lake basin. The best access is from Trout Creek or Noxon, Montana, on the southwest side and from Highway 2 about 20 miles south of Libby, Montana, on the east side.

Wanless Lake from Cabinet Divide Trail No. 360

Trails: Engle Lake, Engle Peak, Wanless Lake, Swamp Creek

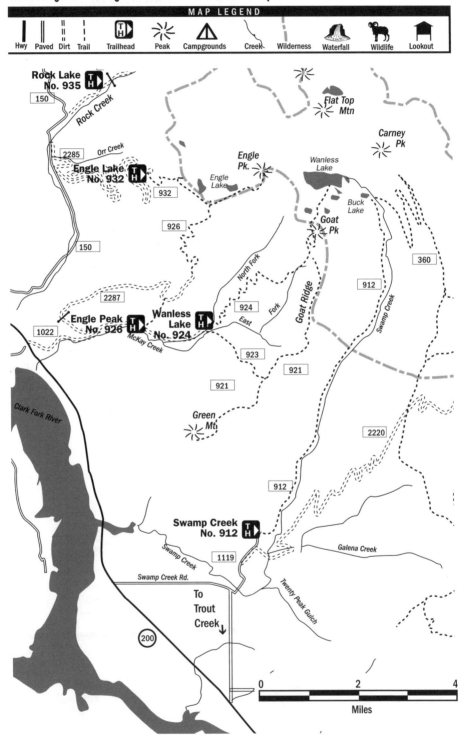

MAP LEGEND

Hwy | Paved | Dirt | Trail | Trailhead | Peak | Campgrounds | Creek | Wilderness | Waterfall | Wildlife | Lookout

Rock Lake No. 935

150

Rock Creek

Flat Top Mtn

Carney Pk

2285 · Orr Creek

Engle Lake No. 932

Engle Pk.

Wanless Lake

932

Engle Lake

Buck Lake

926

Goat Pk

150

360

2287

North Fork

912

924

Wanless Lake No. 924

Goat Ridge

Engle Peak No. 926

Fork

East

Swamp Creek

1022

McKay Creek

923

921

921

Green Mtn

2220

912

Swamp Creek No. 912

Galena Creek

Swamp Creek

1119

Swamp Creek Rd.

To Trout Creek

200

Twenty Peak Gulch

Clark Fork River

0   2   4

Miles

Engle Lake Trail No. 932 and Engle Peak Trail No. 926

Destination: Engle Lake, Engle Peak, 7,583 feet. *Map, page 60.*

USGS Map: Goat Peak

Trailhead: To reach Trail No. 932, turn off Highway 200 near milepost 17 about 2 miles east of Noxon, Montana, onto Rock Creek Road No. 150; proceed about 4 miles to Orr Creek Road No. 2285, veer right and follow it about 7 miles to a gate and parking area. To reach Trail No. 926 turn off Highway 200 near milepost 18 about 3 miles east of Noxon onto McKay Creek Road No. 1022 (opposite the turnoff to Noxon Rapids Dam); proceed about 3 miles to the signed trailhead on the left.

Chris Savage fishing Engle Lake

Trail Length: No. 932 begins on Orr Creek Road No. 2285 and covers nearly 4 miles to Engle Lake. On the ridgeline above the lake, the trail forks: 932 bears left and down into the lake basin and 926 bears right and up to Engle Peak. No. 926 begins on McKay Creek Road No. 1022 and climbs for a mile or so to Forest Service Road No. 2287, where it cuts a switchback, then climbs steeply to the ridge top. There it joins trail No. 932 after about 4.5 miles altogether.

Trail Conditions: Both are in good shape.

Elevation Gain: No. 932 gains about 1,500 feet to the top of a ridge in the first mile and a half, then later descends more than 400 feet to the lake. Where the trail drops into the lake basin, a fork carries on to Engle Peak for about another 1,000 feet. No. 926 climbs for 3,700 feet to its junction with Trail

No. 932, which makes for some 4,800 feet altogether to the top of Engle Peak.

Estimated Duration of Hike: No. 932 takes about 3 to 4 hours up and 2 to 3 hours down. No. 926 takes about 4 to 5 hours up and 3 to 4 hours down. Either trail can be done in a day, but the best way to enjoy this part of the Cabinet Mountains Wilderness is to plan for an overnight stay at the lake.

Sweat Index: strenuous

Best Features: alpine lake, fishing, spectacular rugged mountain views, close-up look at the effects of a forest fire in 2000.

Availability of Water Along the Trail: none on Trail No. 932 and none from near the bottom on No. 926

Stream Crossings: none

What's it like? Engle Lake and Engle Peak are among the premier destinations for wilderness enthusiasts in the Cabinet Mountains. The lake nestles in a glaciated cirque and is the largest of seven lakes in the basin. It harbors a feisty population of small cutthroat trout. The peak, at 7,583 feet, is one of the easiest to climb because of a switchbacking trail up its southwest flank. The rocky summit is above tree line and is exposed to what is usually a stiff, cool breeze or the brutal glare of the sun on hot summer days.

Trail No. 932 begins in an old clear-cut that has reforested and is now a dynamic stand of young, vigorous timber. The trail is often quite steep in the first mile or so, but once on the ridgeline it gently undulates with the terrain. A massive wind-storm in the late 1990s toppled thousands of trees, and then in 2000 a wildfire raced to the top of the ridge. The trail traverses this burned area, offering a first-hand look at the effects of fire in a high-elevation forest. Farther along the ridge, the trail skirts some rocky overhangs that afford spectacular views to the north. Views out over the Clark Fork Valley to the south can also be enjoyed along the way. Trail No. 926 spends a great deal of time in the trees and twice ties in with old roads and skid trails. Hunters utilize it a lot, but the majority of hikers will use No. 932 to access Engle Lake and Engle Peak.

Camping: Several primitive campsites are located at the lake.

Precautions: The junction of Trails 932 and 926 can be confusing because of the signage. If coming in on No. 932 and you are headed for the peak, don't fol-low the sign that says "Engle Peak Trail 926" with an arrow pointed downhill. The trail to the peak does go downhill at one point to get around a large boulder field, but this junction is not the place. A bear den has been identified adjacent to the trail climbing Engle Peak not far beyond where Trail 932 drops into the lake. Avoid the area in the early spring when bears are emerging from their dens, or use extreme caution when hiking in this vicinity.

Alternate Hikes: Some great bushwhacking awaits the adventurous hiker, espe-cially in the Engle Lake basin. Six other lakes and some fabulous, expansive rock slabs beg to be explored. Beware the notion of hiking from the top of Engle Peak to Wanless Lake, only a mile or so to the east; the terrain is exceedingly rugged.

Wanless Lake Trail No. 924

Destination: Wanless Lake, Upper Lakes. *Map, page 60.*

USGS Map: Noxon Rapids Dam, Goat Peak

Trailhead: Opposite the turnoff to Noxon Rapids Dam on Montana Highway 200, near milepost 18, turn east onto McKay Creek Road No. 1022 and go 4 miles to the trailhead.

Trail Length: 9 miles one-way

Trail Condition: good

Elevation Gain: 3,500 feet to Tacklebox Pass and descend 1,400 feet to Wanless Lake

Estimated Duration of Hike: 5 to 7 hours up, 4 to 5 hours down

Sweat Index: strenuous

Best Features: alpine lakes, rugged peaks, good fishing, wildlife

Availability of Water Along the Trail: A couple of streams cross the trail, though the second one may only be a trickle late in the year.

Stream Crossings: one major stream crossing less than a mile above the trailhead via a footbridge

What's it like? Long, sweeping switchbacks lead high into the East Fork of McKay Creek beneath the shadow of Goat Peak (6,889 feet). It's a sprawling, open basin that is home to mule deer and elk. The trail descends a steep, rocky face where, the way an outfitter once told the story, a packhorse was lost when the tackle boxes on its sides shifted and caused the animal to fall over the edge; hence the name Tacklebox Pass. Once off the talus and below the rockslide, the trail passes near several small lakes referred to as the Upper Lakes, at least one of which has a healthy population of cutthroat trout. The real destination, though, for the vast majority of people on this trail is Wanless Lake, the largest lake in the CMW. It also teems with some of the largest trout in the wilderness. It is a mile long and over a quarter mile from shore to shore at its widest point. The cirque cradling this lake is a giant basin that once pushed a massive alpine glacier into the Clark Fork Valley far below.

Camping: Numerous primitive campsites have been used over the years by hikers and horsemen seeking the solitude of this spectacular lake. More adventuresome hikers might seek the far west end of the lake for even remoter campsites.

Alternate Hikes: A scramble down a 600-foot talus slope near Wanless Lake will connect Trail No. 924 with Swamp Creek Trail No. 912 at Buck Lake. Trail 924 also connects with Goat Ridge Trail No. 921 which in turn connects with Bearpaw Trail No. 923 and makes for a nice loop hike of about 13 or 14 miles. Trail 921 continues out to Green Mountain, the top of which burned in 2000.

Swamp Creek Trail No. 912

Destination: Buck Lake, Lost Buck Pass. *Map, page 60.*

USGS Map: Goat Peak

Trailhead: 5 miles east of Noxon, Montana, near milepost 20 on Highway 200, turn east onto Swamp Creek Road and travel about 2.5 miles. The main road bends to the south (right), but take the sharp turn north (left) and follow this road nearly 2 miles to the trailhead at the end of the road.

Buck Lake at the headwaters of Swamp Creek

Trail Length: 13 miles one-way

Trail Condition: good

Elevation Gain: 2,500 feet to the lake

Estimated Duration of Hike: 6 to 7 hours up, 5 to 6 hours down

Sweat Index: strenuous

Best Features: classic U-shaped glacial valley, lots of beaver activity, alpine lake

Availability of Water Along the Trail: The trail closely follows Swamp Creek much of the way.

Stream Crossings: a minor crossing at Goat Creek and another a mile or so below the lake

What's it like? From the parking area, take the trail down into the stream bottom. You will pass beneath a BPA power line and begin the long journey up Swamp Creek. Most of the trail enjoys a gentle grade. On the one side you will observe beaver ponds and perhaps see a moose, while on the other will be the cliffs and rock spires of Goat Ridge. In places it is possible to detect the action of the glacier as it ground against rock on its way down the valley thousands of years ago. Look for glacial striations in the bedrock where it surfaces. The trail crosses numerous areas of talus rock. Buck Lake sits in a luxuriant meadow full of brush, grasses and wildflowers. It is a small, shallow lake, yet still holds a bunch of tiny cutthroats.

Camping: A popular destination for horsemen and hikers; care needs to be exercised in selecting a campsite so impacts are minimized in this fragile environment. A small primitive campsite is located on the southeast shore of the lake.

Alternate Hikes: Trail 912 continues from Buck Lake up to Lost Buck Pass where it connects with Cabinet Divide Trail No. 360 and with Geiger Lakes Trail No. 656, see map, page 65. Claw your way through thick brush and scramble up a 600-foot-high talus slope to get to Wanless Lake from Buck Lake.

Trails: Bramlet Lake, Geiger Lakes, Cabinet Divide, Iron Meadow, Bear Lakes, Baree Lake, Divide Cutoff

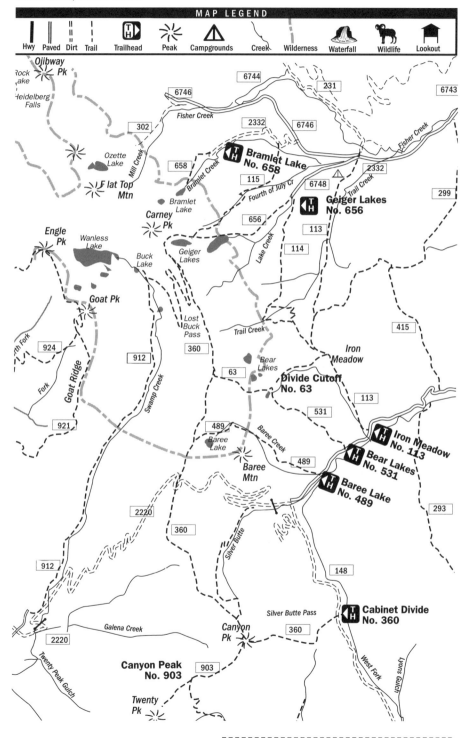

MAP LEGEND

Hwy | Paved | Dirt | Trail | Trailhead | Peak | Campgrounds | Creek | Wilderness | Waterfall | Wildlife | Lookout

Bramlet Lake Trail No. 658

Destination: Bramlet Lake. *Map, page 65.*

USGS Map: Howard Lake

Trailhead: About 17 miles south of Libby, Montana, turn west off Highway 2 onto West Fisher Creek Road No. 231. Follow it approximately 6 miles and turn west onto Road No. 2332 and proceed past the Lake Creek Campground approximately 3 miles to the trailhead.

Trail Length: 1.5 miles one-way

Trail Condition: The trail is an old, overgrown mining road now maintained for foot and horse access.

Elevation Gain: 800 feet

Estimated Duration of Hike: 1 to 1.5 hours up, 30 minutes to 1 hour down

Sweat Index: easy

Best Features: alpine lake

Availability of Water Along the Trail: none

Stream Crossings: none

Bramlet Lake

What's it like? The trail into Bramlet Lake is one of the easiest hikes in the CMW. The wilderness boundary, in fact, is right at the mouth of the lake. The trail follows an old mining road all the way to the very outlet of the lake, though the road is overgrown now and maintained as a trail. Beyond the dark forest lining the lower lake's western shoreline is a steeply ascending slope to another small lake. Both the lower and upper lakes are in a serene, forested setting, and the lower lake harbors fish.

Camping: Primitive campsites can be found at the lower lake.

Alternate Hikes: The half-mile hike to Upper Bramlet Lake requires bushwhacking and about a 400-foot climb. It is also possible to cross-country hike to the Geiger Lakes basin for an interesting loop with Fourth of July Creek Trail No. 115.

Geiger Lakes Trail No. 656

Destination: Geiger Lakes and Lost Buck Pass. *Map, page 65.*

USGS Map: Goat Peak

Trailhead: About 17 miles south of Libby, Montana, turn west off Highway 2 onto West Fisher Creek Road No. 231. Follow it approximately 6 miles and turn south onto Road No. 6748; proceed about 2 miles to the trailhead.

Trail Length: 2 miles to the lower lake, 3 miles to the upper lake, 4 miles to the pass

Trail Condition: excellent

Elevation Gain: 1,000 feet to the lower lake, 1,600 feet to the upper lake, 2,200 feet to the pass

Estimated Duration of Hike: 1 to 2 hours to the lakes, 2 to 3 hours to the pass and anywhere from 1 to 3 hours back down.

Sweat Index: moderate

Best Features: alpine lakes

Availability of Water Along the Trail: The trail skirts Lake Creek both at its beginning and again at the lower lake.

Stream Crossings: The one stream crossing has a strongly built footbridge.

What's it like? Trail 656 cuts through a young forest of Douglas fir, larch and lodgepole pine on its way to Lower Geiger Lake. A sturdy footbridge crosses the creek near the trail's beginning; a somewhat more rickety footbridge crosses the outlet of the lower lake to several good campsites. The trail climbs the hillside north of the lake, from which there are some splendid views; then it meanders along a gentle ridge to Trail No. 48, the spur trail into Upper Geiger Lake. The lower lake is beautiful, but this lake is absolutely gorgeous. Framed by Carney Peak (7,173 feet) to the northwest and Ferrell's Wall to the southwest, this is a picture-perfect subalpine setting. Continuing on Trail 656 for another mile and a half brings the hiker into Lost Buck Pass. A short jaunt through the pass offers a splendid view of Wanless Lake and the entire Swamp Creek valley.

Camping: Primitive campsites are present at both lakes.

Alternate Hikes: Fourth of July Creek Trail No. 115 ties in with Trail 656 on the ridge above the upper lake; from its trailhead to this junction is approximately 3.5 miles. Trail 656 connects with Cabinet Divide Trail No. 360 at Lost Buck Pass and provides access to the south end of the wilderness. An apparent trail junction in the pass can lead to a route up Carney Peak, a rugged but rewarding climb. A variety of open and closed loop hikes are possible from Geiger Lakes.

Cabinet Divide Trail No. 360

Destination: Cabinet Divide. *Map, page 65.*

USGS Map: Goat Peak, Silver Butte Pass

Trailhead: Geiger Lakes Trail No. 656 connects to this trail at Lost Buck Pass (see the description for Geiger Lakes, page 67, for directions to the trailhead). The southeast end of this trail is outside the wilderness and has a trailhead at Silver Butte Pass. To get there turn off Highway 200 about 2 miles west of Trout Creek, Montana onto the Blue Slide Road and go 4 miles to Vermilion River Road 154. Follow this road approximately 7 miles to Silver Butte Pass Road No. 148 and take it 5 miles to the top of the pass and the trailhead.

Trail Length: 14 miles from Silver Butte Pass to Lost Buck Pass (about 6 miles are within the wilderness)

Trail Condition: good

Elevation Gain: Along that portion of this trail inside the wilderness there is minimal elevation loss or gain, but from Silver Butte Pass to Canyon Peak it is a doozy of a climb for over 2,000 feet.

Estimated Duration of Hike: 6 to 8 hours in either direction

Sweat Index: difficult

Best Features: scenic alpine ridge walking

Availability of Water Along the Trail: none

Stream Crossings: none

What's it like? The Cabinet Divide trail is a connecting trail providing access to Buck Lake, Geiger Lakes, Bear Lakes and Baree Lake. It also extends well beyond the southern terminus of the wilderness and ties in with a trail system in the Vermilion River drainage. The majority of the elevation gain traveling west from Silver Butte Pass is acquired in the initial 2 miles, making that part of the trail a challenging hike. From Canyon Peak (6,326 feet) all the way to Lost Buck Pass (a distance of perhaps 10 miles), the trail undulates with the ridge-top terrain. Spectacular views are plentiful along its entire length. Carney Peak (7,173 feet) towers above the north side of Lost Buck Pass and makes for a challenging climb.

Camping: Spending a night on a ridge top can be an exhilarating experience and this ridgeline offers loads of camping potential.

Precautions: Just remember, there is no water along this ridgeline trail, unless it comes from remnant snow banks early in the season.

Alternate Hikes: Several trails inside and from outside the wilderness connect to this trail including Geiger Lakes Trail 656, Swamp Creek Trail 912, Bear Lakes Trail 531 and Baree Lake Trail 489.

Iron Meadow Trail No. 113

Destination: Iron Meadow. *Map, page 65.*

USGS Map: Silver Butte Pass

Trailhead: At Sedlak Park on Highway 2 about 20 miles south of Libby, Montana, turn south onto Silver Butte Fisher River Road No. 148. Go about 9 miles to the trailhead. Watch for the turn underneath the power lines.

Trail Length: 3 miles one-way

Trail Condition: excellent

Elevation Gain: 900 feet

Estimated Duration of Hike: 2 hours either way

Sweat Index: moderate

Best Features: natural meadows, connections to other trails

Availability of Water Along the Trail: The trail stays high on the hillside above Iron Meadow Creek, which has barely a trickle at the Trail 63 junction.

Stream Crossings: none

What's it like? This gentle trail meanders through a quiet forest, first of nearly all lodgepole pine, then a mix of old-growth trees including spruce, larch, Douglas fir, Western whitepine and subalpine fir. A short ways north of the junction with Trail 63, a small meadow appears through the timber below. This is the start of Iron Meadow, a narrow gap in the forest full of grasses and sedges and other plants and shrubs commonly associated with wetlands. It stretches for several hundred yards between steeply rising hillsides.

Precautions: The trailhead is beneath a large BPA power line and an aggressive noxious weed known as rush skeletonweed has been found here. Extreme caution should be exercised to prevent this plant's spread by hikers or their vehicles.

Camping: not really

Alternate Hikes: Iron Meadow Trail 113 provides access to several other trails, including the Divide Cutoff Trail No. 63 to Bear Lakes, West Fisher Divide Trail No. 6 to Barren Peak and Silver Dollar Trail No. 114, which connects with Geiger Lakes Trail No. 656. Various loop hikes are options in this area.

Bear Lakes Trail No. 531

Destination: Bear Lakes. *Map, page 65.*

USGS Map: Silver Butte Pass, Goat Peak

Trailhead: At Sedlak Park on Highway 2 about 20 miles south of Libby, Montana, turn south onto Silver Butte Fisher River Road No. 148. Go about 10 miles to the trailhead.

Trail Length: 3 miles one-way

Trail Condition: excellent

Elevation Gain: 2,000 feet

Estimated Duration of Hike: 2 to 3 hours up, 1.5 to 2 hours down

Sweat Index: moderate

Best Features: alpine lakes

Lower Bear Lake

Availability of Water Along the Trail: none

Stream Crossings: none

What's it like? Trail 531 appears on some maps, such as the 1992 version of the wilderness map, as Trail 178. It meanders up a forested mountainside to its junction with Trail 63. The first mile or more is through a fascinating forest of almost pure lodgepole pine, which gives way to thick mountain hemlock saplings overtopped by larch. There are three lakes in the Bear Lakes group. A spur trail stemming from Trail 531 accesses the upper lake in a small basin flanked by a low ridge. Not far beyond the upper lake, the trail connects with No. 63 and another spur to the middle lake.

Camping: A primitive campsite is located at the upper lake and another campsite can be found at the middle lake.

Alternate Hikes: Trail 531 ties in with Trail 63 near the middle lake, which connects the Cabinet Divide with Iron Meadow Creek. Iron Meadow Trail 113 connects with Silver Dollar Trail 114, which shares a trailhead with Geiger Lakes Trail 656. A variety of loop hikes can be planned in this area.

Baree Lake Trail No. 489

Destination: Baree Lake. *Map, page 65.*

USGS Map: Silver Butte Pass, Goat Peak

Trailhead: At Sedlak Park on Highway 2 about 20 miles south of Libby, Montana, turn south on Silver Butte Fisher River Road No. 148. Go about 10 miles to the trailhead. It can also be reached from the Clark Fork Valley side of the Cabinets by going up Vermilion River Road No. 154, and near milepost 7, turn north onto Silver Butte Road No. 148. Follow it over Silver Butte Pass for a total of about 8 miles to the trailhead.

Trail Length: 4 miles one-way

Trail Condition: good

Elevation Gain: 2,700 feet

Estimated Duration of Hike: 2 to 3 hours up, 1.5 to 2.5 hours down

Sweat Index: difficult

Best Features: alpine lake, old trapper's cabin

Availability of Water Along the Trail: The trail twice crosses Baree Creek, a perennial stream.

Baree Cabin nestles in the forest surrounding the lake.

Stream Crossings: Both crossings of Baree Creek are easily negotiated.

What's it like? Baree Mountain forms the southern edge of the Cabinet Mountains Wilderness. Below its grassy summit nestles the lake of the same name. The trail up Baree Creek cuts through a young forest and a few open brush fields and offers some fine views of the north side of Baree Mountain, which is a tad over 6,400 feet. The mountain's rounded dome shape boasts some of the most stunning, high-elevation meadows in the Cabinets. A little southeast of the lake, hidden away in an encroaching forest, is an old log cabin. A prospector built it early in the 1900s but apparently failed to strike it rich. The legacy of his passing remains, though the forest is slowly reclaiming the site.

Camping: A primitive campsite is located at the southeast corner of the lake.

Precautions: The old miner's cabin near Baree Lake is in an advanced stage of deterioration and should be cautiously viewed from the outside.

Alternate Hikes: Trail 489 continues from the lake to the Cabinet Divide and connects with Trail 360. A nice loop hike can be made of Baree and Bear lakes, or, for an open loop, go south along Trail 360 to Canyon Peak and then out to Silver Butte Pass.

Divide Cutoff Trail No. 63

Destination: Cabinet Divide, Bear Lakes. *Map, page 65.*

USGS Map: Silver Butte Pass, Goat Peak

Trailhead: Called the Divide Cutoff, this trail connects Iron Meadow Trail 113 with Bear Lakes Trail 531 and Cabinet Divide Trail 360. See the descriptions for each of those trails, pages 68-69, for directions to a trailhead that will access Trail 63.

Trail Length: 3 miles one-way

Trail Condition: good

Elevation Gain: 2,000 feet

Estimated Duration of Hike: 2 hours either way

Sweat Index: moderate

Best Features: old-growth forest, alpine lakes, scenic ridge top

Availability of Water Along the Trail: a few seeps and trickling streams but no good water supply

Stream Crossings: nothing significant

What's it like? From near Iron Meadow, this trail climbs rather steeply through an exquisite forest of old-growth trees. Especially eye-catching are the mammoth spruce and the tall, conical subalpine firs. Nearly the entire length of this trail is graced with this ancient stand of trees. A spur trail accesses Middle Bear Lake, from which the lower and largest of the Bear Lakes can be reached by bushwhacking. Where this trail tops the cliffs behind the middle lake, beautiful alpine meadows and rock fields cloak the broad ridges above all three lakes, and sweeping panoramas afford excellent views of the surrounding mountainous terrain.

Camping: Good campsites are located at the upper and middle lakes of the Bear Lakes group.

Alternate Hikes: Trail 63 is a wonderful connection between the Cabinet Divide and Iron Meadow, as well as Bear Lakes Trail 531. Several loop hikes are possible in this area.

Isabella

Shoulders stooped, feet dragging, too tired to even breathe heavily, I shuffled among the chaotic boulders clumsily scattered across the slope over which I carefully picked my way. I paused on a rocky knob and surveyed the immense country I had put behind me in six hours of hiking, scrambling and sweating. Hayes Ridge descended from the summit of Bald Eagle Peak into the deep valley of the Bull River's east fork. My eyes followed its timbered climb from the shadowy road where I had left the truck back up to the 7,655-foot peak. My feet screamed, "Mercy!" when they realized I was studying the ascent of more than 4,000 vertical feet up which they had carried my ponderous frame. ●

For years I had gazed longingly at the pyramidal spire called Bald Eagle Peak in the heart of the Cabinet Mountains Wilderness, desperately wanting to climb it. You can't miss it when driving Montana Highway 56, if you happen to glance up the East Fork where the highway first crosses the river when headed north. Though just the ninth highest peak in the Cabinets, it is an imposing bastion on the main spine of the range.

Isabella Lake rests on the north slope of Elephant Peak

I was headed into the high country for my annual birthday hike and set my sights on Bald Eagle Peak. As I planned the day-long excursion into the soaring heights of my favorite mountain range, I noticed on the map a small lake that appeared to be a worthy destination just a couple of miles south of the peak. It lay like a jewel in a locket cradled in the bosom of Elephant Peak. The high-elevation basin where snow-fed waters created this liquid gem gave the lake the distinction of being the highest in the range, save one. I anticipated Isabella, at 6,900 feet, to be a spectacular date for lunch.

She was not a disappointment.

An alpine glacier had labored long and hard to sculpt the cirque in which Isabella glistened like a newly cut diamond. I traversed a snowdrift into this alpine sanctuary, a reminder of the glacier that lived here thousands of years ago. Even though late July, it curved westward for several hundred yards and was as much as 20 feet deep. Standing upon that mound of hard-packed snow, I closed my eyes and imagined the power of the ice that clung to the broken sedimentary rock crumbling from the cliffs above, grinding it into the angular stones strung across the moraine like pearls on a necklace.

Topping a gentle rise dotted with ancient sentries of alpine larch, I spied the lake beyond a copse of dwarfed firs. Sparkles of sunlight danced on her rippled surface, and the lapping of water on her shore sounded like children laughing.

I settled into a nest of beargrass and sedges near the water's edge. The wind's soft voice murmured peacefully; its gentle caress wiped my brow with coolness collected from a vast snowfield protected by the shadow of the mountain. I nodded off in the tranquil serenity of Isabella's lap.

I might have slept a thousand years, for all I knew, and dreamed a thousand dreams. The rest was an ointment that soothed more than the sore muscles in my legs; my mind, my soul, my spirit – all that is inside me – was rejuvenated by the toil of the hike, the persistent silence of the mountains and the dreams that transported me into a place of peaceful recuperation.

Upon waking, I found Isabella still clutching me to her side. The trees waved their skeletal arms in greeting, animated by the breeze descending from the crags above the lake. I ate lunch, though the events of the day had already appeased a deeper hunger, which, for me, only the wilderness seems to satisfy.

My appetite was for perspective and in the solitude of the high Cabinets, with the sky, the earth and Isabella Lake as witnesses, I embraced a positive perspective of myself. I knew intuitively that perspective would carry me through the coming days down below where life matters and where the people with whom I share my life inspire me through the simple, everyday tasks of living.

I left Isabella that afternoon ladened with treasures gleaned from that rendezvous in the high country. Children laughed, sunbeams danced and a lullaby played among the peaks. I had had my fill but yearned for more.

Next time. There will always be a next time and once again the opportunity to escape from the drudgery that sometimes defines my life. Isabella agreed to another date, and I hope I am not a disappointment.

Section II:

The West Cabinets

The Lay of the Land

Between the Kootenai and Clark Fork rivers, the Bull and Pack rivers, and rising to the northeast above the deep waters of Lake Pend Oreille is a block of mountains most often called the West Cabinets. The Montana-Idaho state line slices through the heart of these mountains. This is the meeting place of two national forests – Montana's Kootenai and Idaho's Kaniksu – and parts of four counties.

Not a lot of the West Cabinets has escaped the incursion of man, but three wild areas remain unspoiled and nearly impenetrable. The Scotchman Peaks in the southern corner of this portion of the range is probably the least-tamed part of the entire Cabinet Mountains range outside the wilderness. At the opposite end of the West Cabinets, occupying the northern tip, are Katka Peak and Clifty Mountain. They rise above some 25 square miles of wild forests and ridges within view of Bonners Ferry, Idaho. Between these two areas is the sprawling wildlands of the Pend Oreille Divide. From Calder Mountain on the north to Rattle Pass on the south, this collection of peaks and lakes and ridges offers some fine hiking opportunities.

Scotchman Peak, left, and Scotchman No. 2

Only one peak in the West Cabinets surpasses 7,000 feet in elevation, and that is Scotchman Peak at 7,009 feet. Its twin to the north, Scotchman No. 2, is a mere 20 feet less in height. Only one other named peak eclipses 6,900 feet, and that is Savage Mountain by a mere two yards. Several of the pinnacles framing the headwall of Ross Creek in a jumble of ragged cliffs called The Compton Crags also exceed 6,900 feet. Ten other named peaks top 6,500 feet.

Though these elevations seem low compared to other mountain ranges in the Rockies, the rugged nature of much of this terrain belies their stature. The Scotchmans are still so wild that the Forest Service has proposed at least part of the area for future inclusion in the wilderness preservation system.

The two largest watersheds draining the West Cabinets are Callahan Creek, which flows to Troy, Montana, and Lightning Creek, which empties into the Clark Fork River at the town of Clark Fork, Idaho. But other important streams such as Boulder, Keeler, Blue, Trestle, Rapid Lightning and Grouse creeks contribute to the variety of terrain found in these mountains.

There are not as many lakes here as in the Cabinet Mountains Wilderness (CMW), but the two largest lakes in the entire range are in this section. Bull Lake lies in the valley separating the West and East Cabinets, but in this sense "East" typically refers to the mountains of the CMW. Though perhaps hydrologically connected to Bull River in a subterranean fashion, Bull Lake is actually fed primarily by Ross Creek and emptied by Lake Creek into the Kootenai River. It is 5 miles long and averages nearly a half-mile wide. Due west of Bull Lake by about 3 miles is Spar Lake. Its deep waters occupy over 400 surface acres.

Another dozen lakes or so are scattered across the West Cabinets, although about half of them are concentrated near the Pend Oreille Divide from Mount Pend Oreille (6,755 feet) to Moose Mountain (6,543 feet).

Perhaps what are the largest trees in the state of Montana are located in the West Cabinets. The stand of ancient cedars known as the Ross Creek Cedar Grove just a few miles off Highway 56 between Noxon and Troy, Montana, harbor trees more than 10 feet in diameter, up to 200 feet tall and estimated to be approaching 1,000 years old. Most of these giants are Western red cedar, but there are also Western hemlock, Western white pine and other species of tremendous dimensions found here.

Access to the West Cabinets begin in the Idaho communities of Bonners Ferry, Naples, Sandpoint, Hope and Clark Fork and from Highway 200 in Montana between Heron and Noxon, as well as north along Highway 56 and Highway 2 to Troy. Close to 60 trails interlace across this section of the range. The Forest Service manages the vast majority of the West Cabinets' landscape.

From Boulder City Ghost Town between Moyie Springs, Idaho, and Troy, Montana, to the active lookout tower atop Squaw Peak near Heron, Montana, the West Cabinets offer a wide variety of recreational opportunities.

Katka-Boulder

The northernmost corner of the Cabinet Mountains contains some of the most scenic country and perhaps the best panoramic vistas throughout the range. It is a small area dominated by two mountainous ridges: Black Mountain-Clifty Mountain-Katka Peak on the north side of Boulder Creek and Iron Mountain-Boulder Mountain-Timber Mountain south and east of Boulder Creek. The primary access route is Road No. 408 that connects Highway 95 near Naples, Idaho, with Boulder City, an abandoned mining settlement, only a couple of miles from the Kootenai River between Moyie Springs, Idaho, and Troy, Montana. From west to east, the road follows Twentymile Creek over Twentymile Pass and continues down Boulder Creek.

The Kootenai River borders this end of the Cabinets on the north, and the magnificent Paradise Valley lies among the foothills tumbling off the mountainsides towards Bonners Ferry, Idaho, to the northwest. There were once more than 100 miles of trails to be explored in this far-north outpost of the Cabinet Mountains, but many of them fell into disuse, were roaded over or are no longer maintained because of limited access. Nonetheless, some great hikes remain, and it is not hard to still find miles and miles of fabulous hiking. This corner of the Cabinets should not be overlooked for great excursions into the high country.

Boulder Mountain, left, looms over Hunt Girl Creek.

Trails: Katka Peak, McGinty Ridge, Iron Mountain, Buck Mountain, East Fork Boulder Creek, Timber Mountain, Kelly Pass, Orville Heath, North Callahan

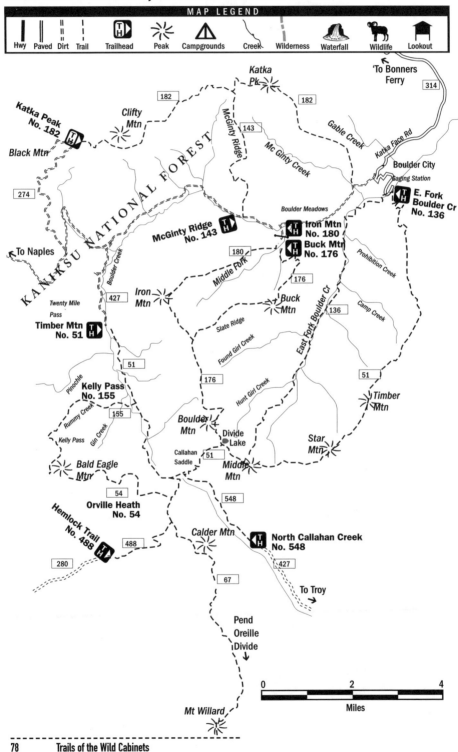

MAP LEGEND

Hwy | Paved | Dirt | Trail | Trailhead | Peak | Campgrounds | Creek | Wilderness | Waterfall | Wildlife | Lookout

To Bonners Ferry

Katka Pk

314

182

182

Clifty Mtn

Katka Peak No. 182

143

Gable Creek

Katka Face Rd

Black Mtn

Boulder City

Gaging Station

274

E. Fork Boulder Cr No. 136

Boulder Meadows

To Naples

McGinty Ridge No. 143

Iron Mtn No. 180

Buck Mtn No. 176

180

Prohibition Creek

Middle Fork

176

427

Iron Mtn

Buck Mtn

136

Camp Creek

Twenty Mile Pass

Slate Ridge

Timber Mtn No. 51

51

Found Girl Creek

East Fork Boulder Cr

51

Pinochle

Kelly Pass No. 155

176

Timber Mtn

Rummy Creek

155

Hunt Girl Creek

Kelly Pass

Gin Creek

Boulder Mtn

Divide Lake

Star Mtn

Callahan Saddle

51

Bald Eagle Mtn

Middle Mtn

54

Orville Heath No. 54

548

Hemlock Trail No. 488

488

Calder Mtn

North Callahan Creek No. 548

280

427

67

To Troy

Pend Oreille Divide

0   2   4

Miles

Mt Willard

Katka Peak Trail No. 182

Destination: Clifty Mountain, 6,705 feet, and Katka Peak, 6,208 feet. *Map, page 78.*

USGS Map: Moyie Springs, Clifty Mountain

Trailhead: A mile north of Naples, Idaho, turn east off Highway 2/95 onto Road No. 408. It is about 10 miles to the junction of Road No. 274, which climbs to Black Mountain Lookout. The trailhead is about 4 miles up that road near a ridge-top switchback.

Trail Length: 4 miles one-way

Trail Condition: good

Elevation Gain: 1,000 feet

Estimated Duration of Hike: 1 to 1.5 hours to Clifty Mountain, about 2 to 3 hours to Katka Peak

Sweat Index: moderate

Best Features: excellent views of the Kootenai River Valley

Availability of Water Along the Trail: none

Stream Crossings: none

What's it like? Beginning on a nice, flat bench on the ridge top, this trail makes a brief steep pitch up to another broad, flat bench before skirting around the south side of Clifty Mountain. But one must make the easy ascent to the peak by simply climbing the relatively gentle slope from the west. The views from the top are magnificent up and down the Kootenai Valley and north into the Purcell Mountains. Look for the towering summits of the Northwest Peaks Scenic Area to the northeast. The trail mostly follows the ridgeline up and over some minor knobs and around others for another 3 miles out to Katka Pass. McGinty Ridge Trail 143 takes off before entering the pass, which is a notch 400 feet deep between two grassy peaks. Trail 182 enters the pass, then swings out around the pleasantly open south slopes of Katka to a spur trail that climbs up the ridge from the east to the summit of Katka Peak. The summit has additional spectacular views of the surrounding countryside.

Camping: Good ridge-top camping, but no water is available.

Alternate Hikes: Trail 182 continues over Katka Peak and down Burro Ridge to Boulder Creek, but it crosses several closed roads along the way. McGinty Ridge Trail 143 joins this trail at Katka Pass. An old trail can still be found coming up from Dobson Creek on the north side of Katka, but it is no longer maintained because of a lack of access at the bottom.

McGinty Ridge Trail No. 143

Destination: Katka Peak, 6,208 feet. *Map, page 78.*

USGS Map: Clifty Mountain

Trailhead: Similar to finding the trailhead for Clifty Mountain and Katka Peak, turn off Highway 2/95 north of Naples and take Road 408 approximately 15 miles. Look for the McGinty Ridge trailhead on the north side of Road 408 about a mile east of where Clifty Creek crosses the road.

Trail Length: 4 miles one-way

Trail Condition: fair to good

Elevation Gain: 3,000 feet

Estimated Duration of Hike: 3 to 4 hours up, 2 to 3 hours down

Sweat Index: strenuous

Best Features: great views of Boulder Creek and the Kootenai River Valley

Availability of Water Along the Trail: A trickle may be available in an unnamed draw the trail crosses.

Stream Crossings: two minor crossings of a rocky draw

What's it like? Portions of this trail are among the steepest around as it climbs about 1,200 feet in the first mile without too many serious switchbacks. But as the valley rapidly falls farther below, the views of Boulder Creek and Iron Mountain to the south become increasingly awesome. Once the trail is on McGinty Ridge, the hiking becomes much easier since two-thirds of the climb is completed in the first mile and a half. This is a heavily timbered slope, but there are enough openings to catch some breathtaking scenery along the way. The trail joins Trail 182 just south of Katka Pass, which leads the short remaining distance to the top of Katka Peak.

A real prize while hiking is to find a shed elk antler.

Camping: not really

Alternate Hikes: This trail ties in with Trail 182 at Katka Pass, which leads westward to Clifty Mountain.

Iron Mountain Trail No. 180

Destination: Iron Mountain, 6,426 feet. *Map, page 78.*

USGS Map: Clifty Mountain, Twentymile Creek

Trailhead: Take County Road 24 east from Bonners Ferry, Idaho, for about 13 miles where it becomes Forest Road No. 314 and continue southeast on that road to its junction with Boulder Creek Road 408. Bear west on Road 408 and follow it for 3 miles to its junction with Road 628. Cross Boulder Creek on Road 628 and almost immediately you will encounter a gate. Just beyond the gate watch for the trailhead sign on the right. It will be the first trailhead sign flanking the Middle Fork Boulder Creek.

Trail Length: 5 miles one-way

Trail Condition: good

Elevation Gain: 3,400 feet

Estimated Duration of Hike: 3 to 4 hours up, 2 to 3 hours down

Sweat Index: strenuous

Best Features: high open ridges and meadows, great views

Availability of Water Along the Trail: none after the Middle Fork along the first mile of trail.

Stream Crossings: none

What's it like? The Iron Mountain trail climbs steeply up the north side of the Middle Fork Boulder Creek through heavy timber. Views are limited at first, but that belies the fantastic scenery to be enjoyed from the bald summit of Iron Mountain. It is the highest peak on the south side of Boulder Creek, and the views of every part of the drainage are remarkable. Most enjoyable is the network of meadows draped over the ridge tops all the way out to Boulder Mountain and beyond. A spur trail accesses the top of the mountain while the main trail turns southeast and joins up with Buck Mountain Trail 176 after about a mile and a half. The south slopes of Clifty Mountain and Katka Peak form the scenic panorama to the north.

Camping: Because water is scarce atop the ridges accessed by this trail, campsites are few, but staying a night in the sprawling meadows draped across Iron Mountain and Boulder Mountain is an enticing proposition. A primitive campsite is located at Divide Lake.

Alternate Hikes: Trail 180 connects to Buck Mountain Trail 176, which carries on out to Boulder Mountain and Divide Lake.

Buck Mountain Trail No. 176

Destination: Boulder Mountain, 6,928 feet. *Map, page 78.*

USGS Map: Clifty Mountain, Twentymile Creek

Trailhead: Follow the same directions for the Iron Mountain Trail 180 trailhead, page 81, but go another 100 yards, give or take, beyond the first trailhead to locate this one.

Trail Length: 8 miles one-way

Trail Condition: good

Elevation Gain: approximately 3,000 feet

Estimated Duration of Hike: 4 to 6 hours up, 3 to 4 hours down

Sweat Index: strenuous

Best Features: high open ridges and great views

Availability of Water Along the Trail: The trail is close to the Middle Fork for a short ways, and then climbs steeply up the ridge to Buck Mountain, where there is no water.

Stream Crossings: none

What's it like? This is a gut-busting climb for the first few miles, but once up on Slate Ridge, the going gets a little easier. From Buck Mountain (5,689 feet) the trail gradually ascends to the top of the ridge connecting Iron Mountain and Boulder Mountain. Much of the trail is in heavy timber, but just west of Buck Mountain, the terrain opens up into vast meadows cloaking the ridges. They afford expansive views of Boulder Creek and the surrounding countryside. To the south is a small lake at the head end of Found Girl Creek, a twin stream to Hunt Girl Creek farther south. The story behind the names of these two creeks speaks for itself.

Camping: As for Trail 180, camping opportunities on the ridgeline are terrific, except there is no water. However, this trail goes to a primitive campsite at Divide Lake.

Alternate Hikes: This trail connects with Iron Mountain Trail 180 and Timber Mountain Trail 51.

East Fork Boulder Creek Trail No. 136

Destination: Middle Mountain, 6,220 feet. *Map, page 78.*

USGS Map: Clifty Mountain

Trailhead: Take County Road 24 east from Bonners Ferry, Idaho, for about 13 miles where it becomes Forest Road No. 314 and continue southeast on that road past its junction with Boulder Creek Road 408. About a mile beyond that junction is the trailhead near the gaging station where the road crosses Boulder Creek.

Trail Length: 8.5 miles one-way

Trail Condition: fair to good

Elevation Gain: 3,700 feet

Estimated Duration of Hike: 5 to 6 hours up, 4 to 5 hours down

Sweat Index: strenuous

Best Features: Old cedar forests, close to streamside much of the way

Availability of Water Along the Trail: East Fork Boulder Creek is seldom far below the trail, except for the last 3 miles.

Stream Crossings: none

What's it like? From near the gaging station outside the ghost town, this trail follows an old roadbed for the first several miles and meanders through a nice forest of mixed conifers on the east side of the stream. Where Found Girl Creek flows into the east fork, the trail crosses Road 628 and continues upstream on the west side of the east fork. It then crosses Hunt Girl Creek and begins to climb the rugged shoulder of Middle Mountain, switchbacking tightly for 1,200 vertical feet to the first of several false summits. Another 1,200 feet must be conquered to reach the top of the mountain. In the higher terrain the trail is more obscure but is frequently marked with rock cairns. It goes over the very top of Middle Mountain and joins Trail 51 on the south slope in a nice meadow with scattered, stunted trees.

Camping: There are no established campsites along this trail, but by using Leave No Trace techniques, there is ample opportunity for backcountry camping all along this trail.

Alternate Hikes: This trail connects to Timber Mountain Trail 51 on Middle Mountain. A loop hike can be followed by taking Trail 51, at its junction with trail 136, north over Star Mountain and Timber Mountain and back toward Boulder City. Another loop hike is possible by taking Trail 51 southwesterly to Divide Lake, then following Trail 176 over Boulder Mountain and down to Road 628.

Timber Mountain Trail No. 51

Destination: Divide Lake, Timber Mountain. *Map, page 78.*

USGS Map: Clifty Mountain, Leonia

Trailhead: The three best ways onto this trail are to follow the directions for East Fork Boulder Creek Trail 136, page 83, but continue a half-mile past that trailhead to Boulder City; from the end of Boulder Creek Road 427 at the northwest end of the trail (take Road 408 from Highway 2/95 a mile north of Naples, Idaho, for about 12 miles to the junction of Road 427 and turn south, then go just over 2 miles to the end of the road); or from North Callahan Creek via Trail No. 548 (see the directions to that trailhead, page 87).

Trail Length: approximately 20 miles one-way

Trail Conditions: varies from fair to excellent

Elevation Gain: approximately 3,000 feet

Estimated Duration of Hike: 10 to 15 hours to hike the trail's entire length, but most people use it as a connector to other trails or go to destinations along its meandering length.

Sweat Index: strenuous

Best Features: subalpine meadows, pretty little lake, fantastic views

Availability of Water Along the Trail: none for most of the way

Stream Crossings: no significant crossings

What's it like? Timber Mountain Trail No. 51 is one of the longest continuously running trails in the Cabinets. From the end where Boulder Creek Road 427 is blocked and converted to a trail to the other end at Boulder City, an old abandoned mining settlement, this trail traverses 20 miles of stream bottoms and ridge tops. From Boulder Meadows, the old road snakes through the forest to the Callahan Saddle just north of Calder Mountain. From there it winds through 25 switchbacks to an interesting plateau at about 5,800 feet where Divide Lake, a small shallow pothole, is perched on a shelf between Boulder and Middle mountains at the head end of Hunt Girl Creek, a tributary to the East Fork Boulder Creek. Heavy timber, alpine meadows and rocky knobs characterize this trail. Timber Mountain is the highest summit it reaches, at 6,395 feet.

Camping: There are great camping opportunities at Boulder Meadows and a primitive campsite can be found at Divide Lake.

Alternate Hikes: Several other trails connect to this trail including East Fork Boulder Creek Trail No. 136 atop Middle Mountain, Buck Mountain Trail No. 176 at Divide Lake, Orville Heath Trail No. 54 from Bald Eagle Mountain and Kelly Pass Trail No. 155 at Rummy Creek. Access to Pend Oreille Divide Trail No. 67 can be found at Callahan Saddle.

Kelly Pass Trail No. 155

Destination: Kelly Pass, Bald Eagle Mountain, 6,098 feet. *Map, page 78.*

USGS Map: Twentymile Creek

Trailhead: From Highway 2/95 north of Naples, Idaho, turn east onto Road 408 and take it about 12 miles to Road 427. Turn south and go just over 2 miles to the end of the road and the trailhead for Timber Mountain Trail 51 at Boulder Meadows. This trail splits off Timber Mountain Trail 51 in the upper Boulder Creek drainage about 2 miles from the end of the open road.

Trail Length: 3.5 miles one-way

Trail Condition: good

Elevation Gain: 2,000 feet

Estimated Duration of Hike: 3 hours up, 2 hours down

Sweat Index: moderate

Best Features: open ridge top meadows, views of the West Cabinets and Selkirks

Availability of Water Along the Trail: The trail closely follows Rummy Creek.

Stream Crossings: must cross Boulder Creek and Rummy Creek

What's it like? The last 5 miles of the Boulder Creek Road 427 have been rehabilitated and converted to a trail. Trail 155 takes off to the west about 2 miles from the trailhead, crosses Boulder Creek and climbs to Kelly Pass. You will notice a spring near the top of the pass, which feeds Rummy Creek. Several trails meet at the pass and Trail 53 strikes off to the south up the broad ridges draped with wonderful open meadows to the rounded summit of Bald Eagle Mountain.

Camping: Good ridge-top camping opportunities abound, though water is scarce.

Alternate Hikes: This trail makes a fine loop hike with Orville Heath Trail No. 54 and Trail 51.

Orville Heath Trail No. 54

Destination: Bald Eagle Mountain. *Map, page 78.*

USGS Map: Twentymile Creek

Trailhead: Follow the directions to Timber Mountain Trail 51 via Road 408 and Road 427, page 84. This trail can also be reached from North Callahan Trail 548 (see directions, page 87).

Trail Length: 3 miles one-way

Trail Condition: good

Elevation Gain: approximately 1,000 feet

Estimated Duration of Hike: about 2 hours from Callahan Saddle to Bald Eagle Mountain

Sweat Index: moderate

Best Features: access to ridge-top meadows and fantastic views of the West Cabinets and Selkirks

Availability of Water Along the Trail: none

Stream Crossings: none

What's it like? Orville Heath was a rancher who once ran livestock on the high, bald knobs of the West Cabinets. The trail that now sports his name fell into disrepair, but in recent years the Forest Service has reopened it; now it offers a dandy hike to Bald Eagle Mountain either from North Callahan Creek or Boulder Creek. Much of the trail meanders across beautiful meadows and climbs among the gently rising shoulders of the peak to a summit that boasts an incredible view of the valley from Bonners Ferry to McArthur Lake and of the Selkirk Mountains to the west.

Camping: There is a primitive campsite on Callahan Saddle, great camping at Boulder Meadows, and with plenty of water, camping can be enjoyed at the summit of Bald Eagle Mountain.

Alternate Hikes: This trail is part of a nice loop hike utilizing Timber Mountain Trail 51 and Kelly Pass Trail 155. It also connects with Pend Oreille Divide Trail 67.

North Callahan Creek Trail No. 548

Destination: Boulder-Callahan Saddle. *Map, page 78.*

USGS Map: Twentymile Creek, Clifty Mountain

Trailhead: On the south edge of Troy, Montana, turn west off Highway 2 onto Callahan Creek Road No. 427 and go 16 miles to the trailhead.

Trail Length: 4 miles one-way

Trail Condition: excellent

Elevation Gain: approximately 800 feet

Estimated Duration of Hike: 2 hours up, 2 hours or less down

Sweat Index: moderate

Best Features: This trail enters a small but impressive rocky gorge with cascades and pools about 2 miles or so up.

Availability of Water Along the Trail: This trail crosses numerous small draws with running water.

Stream Crossings: Immediately at the trailhead you must negotiate North Callahan Creek, but after that the stream crossings either have bridges or are insignificant.

What's it like? The first mile and a half of this trail follows an old logging road, and then the trail climbs gradually to the Boulder-Callahan saddle. Its gentle grade meanders through the forest, in and out of numerous draws, a few of which are fairly deep, and ties in with other trails on top.

North Callahan Creek Trail provides good access to Divide Lake.

Camping: There is a good campsite at the trailhead.

Alternate Hikes: This trail is actually a connector to a much larger system of trails. It ties in with Timber Mountain Trail 51, which is the best way to Divide Lake.

Pend Oreille Divide

Splitting the West Cabinets in half is a series of peaks connected by a subalpine ridge called the Pend Oreille Divide, the crowning summit of which is Mount Pend Oreille, 6,755 feet. Stretching from Rattle Pass in the south to Calder Mountain in the north, this linear collection of wild country encompasses more than 70,000 acres of primitive uplands sprawled along 20 miles of superb high country. Scattered along the way are numerous small lakes teeming with feisty fish. A terrific network of trails provides access to most of this terrain. Primary roads leading to the trailheads for the Pend Oreille Divide include Lightning Creek Road No. 419, Trestle Creek Road No. 275, Grouse Creek Road No. 280 and Callahan Creek Road No. 427.

The trail to Mount Pend Oreille

Trails: Pend Oreille Divide, Lake Darling, Gem Lake, Moose Lake, Blacktail Lake, Lake Estelle

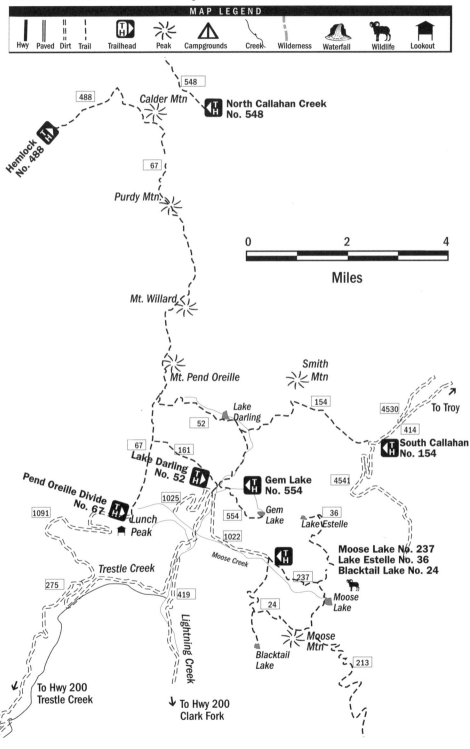

MAP LEGEND

Hwy | Paved | Dirt | Trail | Trailhead | Peak | Campgrounds | Creek | Wilderness | Waterfall | Wildlife | Lookout

548

488

Calder Mtn

North Callahan Creek No. 548

Hemlock No. 488

67

Purdy Mtn

0   2   4

Miles

Mt. Willard

Mt. Pend Oreille

Smith Mtn

154

4530 — To Troy

Lake Darling

52

414

South Callahan No. 154

67   161

Lake Darling No. 52

4541

Pend Oreille Divide No. 67

1025

Gem Lake No. 554

1091

Lunch Peak

554

Gem Lake

36

Lake Estelle

1022

**Moose Lake No. 237
Lake Estelle No. 36
Blacktail Lake No. 24**

Moose Creek

Trestle Creek

275

419

237

24

Moose Lake

Lightning Creek

Blacktail Lake

Moose Mtn

213

↙ To Hwy 200
Trestle Creek

↓ To Hwy 200
Clark Fork

Pend Oreille Divide Trail No. 67

Destination: Pend Oreille Divide. *Map, page 89.*

USGS Map: Mount Pend Oreille, Clark Fork

Trailhead: The most popular jumping off point onto Trail 67 is at Lunch Peak. Turn east off Highway 200 between Hope, Idaho, and Pack River onto Trestle Creek Road No. 275, go 12 miles to Road 1091, and follow it north 4 miles to Lunch Peak Lookout and the trailhead.

Trail Length: 15 miles one-way

Trail Conditions: varies from good to excellent

Elevation Gain: undulates between 5,000 feet and 6,755 feet

Estimated Duration of Hike: From Lunch Peak, the primary destination is Mount Pend Oreille 4 miles away. Round trip could take 4 to 5 hours. To hike the entire length of the trail requires 6 to 8 hours one way.

Sweat Index: moderate to difficult

Best Features: alpine meadows, rugged peaks, spectacular vistas of both the Cabinet and Selkirk mountains

Availability of Water Along the Trail: none

Stream Crossings: none

What's it like? The Pend Oreille Divide not only grants scenic vistas of distant mountains; it is in itself a wonderfully beautiful array of rocky peaks, grassy meadows and lovely forested ridges. From Lunch Peak the trail drops to the saddle above Lake Darling before climbing nearly 600 feet to the summit of Mount Pend Oreille. A spur trail forks off the main trail about a quarter-mile from the junction of Trails 52 and 67 and climbs steeply to the peak. Once on top watch for the old telegraph wire crossing the trail. The south and west slopes of Mount Pend Oreille are characterized by carpets of meadow grasses and high-country wildflowers. Between Mount Pend Oreille and Mount Willard, the trail traverses the headwall of South Callahan Creek, a vast expanse of roadless wild country harboring a spectacular forest of fir and spruce. The northeast side of South Callahan on the flank of Smith Mountain (6,510 feet) was burned extensively in 1994. South of Mount Willard (6,536 feet), Trail 67 drops off the ridgeline and cuts across its shadowy northwest side rather than going over its rugged peak. From where it rejoins the main ridge, the trail then meanders through some of the most beautiful meadows in the Cabinets over Purdy Mountain (6,062 feet) and Calder Mountain (5,699 feet).

Camping: Because water is nearly nonexistent on the ridge, most campers will stay at places off the ridgeline trail such as Lake Darling.

Alternate Hikes: Other trails accessing Pend Oreille Divide Trail 67 include Trail 488 in Grouse Creek, Trail 548 in North Callahan Creek, and Trail 154 in South Callahan Creek via Trail 52 from Lake Darling.

Lake Darling Trail No. 52

Destination: Lake Darling. *Map, page 89.*

USGS Map: Mount Pend Oreille

Trailhead: Between Pack River and Hope, Idaho, turn east off Highway 200 onto Trestle Creek Road No. 275 and travel 16 miles to Lightning Creek Road 419; turn north on 419 and go less than a mile to the trailhead.

Trail Length: 2 miles one-way

Trail Conditions: excellent

Elevation Gain: 600 feet

Estimated Duration of Hike: 1 to 2 hours to Lake Darling

Sweat Index: easy

Best Features: alpine lake

Availability of Water Along the Trail: The trail closely follows upper Lightning Creek all the way to the lake.

Lake Darling and Mount Pend Oreille

Stream Crossings: none, but watch for marshy areas

What's it like? The hike to Lake Darling is great for almost anyone of any hiking capability. This wide, gentle grade wends its way through a pleasant subalpine forest of spruce and fir to a scenic crossing over a sedge-lined pool with the lake framed by conical silhouettes of subalpine fir beyond. The scenic backdrop to the lake is dominated by Mount Pend Oreille. Lake Darling is the headwaters source of Lightning Creek.

Camping: Several primitive campsites can be found near the lake.

Precautions: Lake Darling is known for its squadrons of mosquitoes in the summer. It also has soft, marshy banks, so be careful not to trample the fragile meadows around the edges of the lake. Moose are known to frequent this area.

Alternate Hikes: Trail 52 carries on beyond Lake Darling for another 2 miles or so to its junction with Trail 67 and a nice jaunt to Mount Pend Oreille. A nice loop hike can be completed by proceeding from Lake Darling to Pend Oreille Divide Trail 67, then traveling south for about a mile to its junction with Gordon Creek Trail 161 and back to the trailhead. That loop covers about 7 miles. Lake Darling can also be accessed from South Callahan Creek on Trail 154. Take Road 427 near Troy, Montana, off Highway 2 to Roads 414 and 4541 to the trailhead. This 3-mile-long path ties in with Trail 52 less than a half mile from the lake.

Gem Lake Trail No. 554

Destination: Gem Lake. *Map, page 89.*

USGS Map: Mount Pend Oreille

Trailhead: Between Pack River and Hope, Idaho, turn east off Highway 200 onto Trestle Creek Road 275 and travel 16 miles to Lightning Creek Road 419; turn north on 419 and go about 1.5 miles to the trailhead.

Trail Length: 1.5 miles one-way

Trail Conditions: good

Elevation Gain: 1,200 feet

Estimated Duration of Hike: 1 to 2 hours up, an hour or less down

Sweat Index: moderate

Best Features: alpine lake, scenic views of the Lightning Creek drainage

Availability of Water Along the Trail: Some trickles cross the trail.

Stream Crossings: no significant crossings

Gem Lake

What's it like? This short trail climbs moderately steeply through a forest of mixed species to a boulder field just above the lake's east side. The best panoramic view of the lake and the high ridges and peaks to the west are enjoyed from this boulder field by scrambling up as far as you can go.

Camping: A primitive campsite is located near the lake.

Alternate Hikes: A rugged, off-trail hike connects this lake with Lake Estelle just over the divide to the east.

Moose Lake Trail No. 237

Destination: Moose Lake. *Map, page 89.*

USGS Map: Mount Pend Oreille

Trailhead: Between Pack River and Hope, Idaho, turn east off Highway 200 onto Trestle Creek Road 275 and travel 16 miles to Lightning Creek Road 419; turn north on 419 and go past the spur road to Lake Darling Trail 52 for another mile to Moose Creek Road 1022. Take that road 2 miles to the trailhead, which is shared by Lake Estelle, Blacktail Lake and Moose Lake trails.

Trail Length: 2 miles one-way

Trail Conditions: excellent

Elevation Gain: 400 feet

Estimated Duration of Hike: 1 to 2 hours up, an hour down

Sweat Index: easy

Best Features: beautiful lake, possible wildlife viewing (moose)

Availability of Water Along the Trail: The trail closely follows Moose Creek most of the way to the lake.

Stream Crossings: one minor crossing

What's it like? This hike to Moose Lake is an easy wander through a forested environment. The lake is surrounded by beautiful rocky ridges that offer some great off-trail bushwhacking for the adventurous hiker.

Camping: A primitive campsite is located at the end of the trail near the lake.

Precautions: As with other lakes in the area, watch for wildlife, particularly moose, and be prepared for mosquitoes in the summer. Also take care along the lake's fragile shoreline as the vegetation can be easily trampled and the ground eroded.

Moose Lake

Alternate Hikes:
Trail 213, which is not well maintained, connects Moose Lake with Rattle Creek Road 473 by going over the top of Moose Mountain (6,543 feet).

Blacktail Lake Trail No. 24

Destination: Blacktail Lake. *Map, page 89.*

USGS Map: Mount Pend Oreille

Trailhead: See description for Moose Lake Trail, page 93.

Trail Length: 3 miles one-way

Trail Condition: good

Elevation Gain: 800 feet

Estimated Duration of Hike: 1.5 to 2.5 hours up, 1 to 2 hours down

Sweat Index: difficult

Best Features: alpine lake, wildlife (especially moose)

Availability of Water Along the Trail: none

Stream Crossings: None after initially crossing Moose Creek, though lots of marshy areas occur along the trail.

What's it like? Several miles of hiking through a beautiful forest are high-lighted by a significant amount of boardwalk. The Forest Service has provided wooden planking across many of the spots where the trail traverses wet, marshy areas. A pleasant meadow wraps around the north side of the lake while a boul-der field tumbles to the lake's southwest edge. An active avalanche chute has

pushed tons of debris to the lake's south shore. Blacktail Lake is the headwaters source for Deer Creek, a small tributary to Lightning Creek.

Camping: A primitive campsite is located near the lake on the edge of the meadow bordering the lake's north shore.

Precautions: As with all of the lakes in this area, mosquitoes and other bugs can be real nuisances in the summer; beware of encounters with wildlife, particularly moose; and tread carefully around the lake, as its shoreline is marshy and fragile.

Alternate Hikes: Off-trail hiking opportunities are possible on the ridges surrounding Blacktail Lake.

Boardwalk to Blacktail Lake

Lake Estelle Trail No. 36

Destination: Lake Estelle. *Map, page 89.*

USGS Map: Mount Pend Oreille

Trailhead: See description for Moose Lake Trail, page 93.

Trail Length: 3 miles one-way

Trail Condition: good

Elevation Gain: 500 feet

Estimated Duration of Hike: 1 to 2 hours up, 1 to 2 hours down

Sweat Index: moderate

Best Features: beautiful alpine lake, scenic vistas

Availability of Water Along the Trail: Once out of Moose Creek, there is no water along this trail.

Stream Crossings: none

What's it like? A half a mile or so along Moose Lake Trail 237 is a fork in the trail. Trail 36 to Lake Estelle bears left and gently climbs over a low divide. Though this hike begins in the Lightning Creek drainage, Lake Estelle is actually located in the

Lake Estelle

Lost Creek tributary to South Callahan Creek. The vast majority of the Cabinet Mountains is geologically characterized by sedimentary rock, but along this trail you will notice the presence of granite as well. This is one of the few places in the Cabinets where granite is exposed. The lake is a fine, sparkling body of water framed by a high cliff on the southwest and steeply ascending meadows on the northwest.

Camping: A small, primitive campsite is located next to the lake on its eastern shore.

Alternate Hikes: An interesting cross-country hike lies over the ridge between Lake Estelle and Gem Lake, though it is not a particularly easy route to follow.

Trails: Bee Top-Round Top, Bee Top, Strong Creek

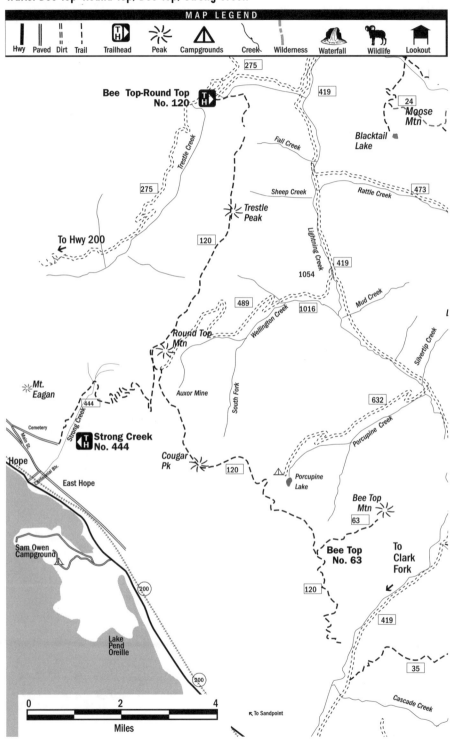

MAP LEGEND

Hwy | Paved | Dirt | Trail | Trailhead | Peak | Campgrounds | Creek | Wilderness | Waterfall | Wildlife | Lookout

275

419

Bee Top-Round Top
No. 120

24 Moose Mtn

Fall Creek

Blacktail Lake

275

Sheep Creek

Rattle Creek

473

Trestle Creek

To Hwy 200

Trestle Peak

120

Lightning Creek

419

1054

489

1016

Mud Creek

Round Top Mtn

Wellington Creek

Silvertip Creek

Mt. Eagan

Auxor Mine

South Fork

632

444

Porcupine Creek

Cemetery

Strong Creek
No. 444

Cougar Pk

120

Porcupine Lake

Bee Top Mtn

63

Hope

Main St.

East Hope

Centennial Blv.

Sam Owen
Campground

Bee Top
No. 63

To
Clark
Fork

200

120

Lake
Pend
Oreille

419

200

35

0   2   4

Miles

↖ To Sandpoint

Cascade Creek

Bee Top-Round Top Trail No. 120

Destination: Bee Top-Round Top, Trestle Peak, 6,320 feet. *Map, page 96.*

USGS Map: Mount Pend Oreille, Elmira

Trailhead: The most popular starting point on this trail is reached by turning off Highway 200 about 12 miles east of Sandpoint, Idaho onto Trestle Creek Road No. 275, between Pack River and Hope, Idaho, and traveling approximately 13 miles to the trailhead, which is located on a switchback about a mile past the junction of Lunch Peak Road No. 1091. Another trailhead is located at the end of Wellington Creek Road No. 489 just south of Round Top Mountain. That trailhead is accessed via Trestle Creek Road 275 and Lightning Creek Road 419. The total distance from Highway 200 to the Wellington trailhead is approximately 30 miles.

Trail Length: 19 miles one-way

Trail Conditions: good to excellent

Elevation Gain: 1,200 feet at highest point

Estimated Duration of Hike: Depending on the destination, this trail can be traveled for anywhere from 2 to 12 hours one-way.

Sweat Index: moderate to strenuous

Best Features: unparalleled views of Lake Pend Oreille, the city of Sandpoint and the West Cabinets

Availability of Water Along the Trail: none

Stream Crossings: none

What's it like? Could it be argued that this is one of the most scenic trails in the world? Yes, because of the extraordinary vistas of Lake Pend Oreille. From almost anywhere along this trail there are outstanding views of Lake Pend Oreille, but especially from Round Top Mountain (6,153 feet) and Cougar Peak (5,983 feet). To reach the highest point along this ridge system requires a brief but moderately rugged climb to the top of Trestle Peak (6,320 feet) for magnificent views in every direction.

Camping: Typical ridgeline camping is available in many places along this trail in numerous primitive sites suitable for pitching a tent or sleeping out under the stars.

Precautions: Trail 120 at its southern end has no right-of-way across private property, so taking it beyond the junction of Bee Top Trail 63 is not advised.

Alternate Hikes: This trail can also be reached by taking Strong Creek Trail No. 444 from the town of East Hope. Trail 444 is an old road all the way to the top and ties in with Trail 120 at the Wellington Creek Road. It is a popular route for mountain bikes. Bee Top Trail 63 provides easy access to the summit of Bee Top Mountain (6,212 feet). A spur trail extends west by southwest beyond Round Top to Eagen Mountain and some fine views of the lake. It drops almost 900 feet over a distance of about 3 miles.

Bee Top Trail No. 63 _ _ _ _

Destination: Bee Top, 6,212 feet. *Map, page 96.*

USGS Map: Clark Fork

Trailhead: Bee Top Trail 63 veers off Bee Top-Round Top Trail No. 120 on the high ridges above the town of Clark Fork. The only way to get there is to follow Trail 120 to the trail junction, or bushwhack up from Porcupine Lake, which is at the end of Porcupine Creek Road 632. That road can be accessed by taking Trestle Creek Road 275 off Highway 200 between Pack River and Hope, Idaho to Lightning Creek Road 419 for a total distance of about 20 miles.

Trail Length: 2.5 miles one-way

Trail Condition: fair to good

Elevation Gain: 400 feet

Estimated Duration of Hike: Once on Trail 63, it only takes an hour or so to get out to Bee Top.

Looking out across Lightning Creek at Bee Top

Sweat Index: moderate

Best Features: terrific views of Lightning Creek, Lake Pend Oreille and the Clark Fork River delta; excellent ridgeline hiking in grassy meadows and rocky openings

Availability of Water Along the Trail: none

Stream Crossings: none

What's it like? Getting to Trail 63 is a bit tricky, or just a lengthy undertaking, but once there, what a grand hike this is out to Bee Top. Aside from a moderate climb of about 300 feet at the beginning, the trail follows this narrow, gently undulating ridge out to a perch on Bee Top's rocky knob that affords a view sure to make you gasp in awe. You can glimpse Still Lake in a small basin on the north side and see far up Lightning Creek. To the east the Scotchman Peaks raise their rugged heads to the sky, but the real treat is the panoramic vista of the pastoral setting of the Clark Fork River delta and Lake Pend Oreille. Both sides of Bee Top and its ridgeline are exceedingly steep and rugged.

Precautions: Lightning Creek Road 419 can be traveled from the town of Clark Fork, but about 6 miles upstream the road is washed out where it crosses East Fork Creek. High water makes it nearly impossible to negotiate, but in late summer and fall 4WD vehicles can make it across successfully.

Alternate Hikes: This trail is an extension of Trail 120.

Strong Creek Trail No. 444

Destination: Round Top, 6,153 feet. *Map, page 96.*

USGS Map: Mount Pend Oreille, Elmira

Trailhead: The trailhead in the town of Hope, Idaho, is a bit obscure. Turn north off Highway 200 onto Centennial Avenue next to Hope's Memorial Community Center. Take a left onto the old highway and go about one-quarter mile to the Post Office. Main Street, a narrow, one-lane paved road, veers right uphill in front of the Post Office. Follow it a couple of hundred yards and take a sharp right uphill toward the cemetery; continue past the cemetery on a dirt road beyond the sign that says "Road Closed ¾ Mile Ahead" to the trailhead.

Trail Length: 7 miles one-way

Trail Condition: excellent

Elevation Gain: 2,700 feet

Estimated Duration of Hike: 4 to 5 hours up on foot, 3 to 4 hours down; a great 1- to 2-hour ride up on a bike and less than an hour down.

Sweat Index: difficult

Best Features: a great trail suitable for mountain bikes, fantastic views from the top

Availability of Water Along the Trail: Strong Creek flows year-round and parallels the first couple miles of the trail.

Stream Crossings: one crossing about 2 miles up

What's it like? Miners explored a lot of this country years and years ago, then left the road in place for future users. It is now maintained as a trail. It climbs steadily through dark timber along the stream to the more open upper slopes, switchbacking from the stream crossing up 2,200 vertical feet to a saddle between Round Top and the Auxor Mine. Views on the way up are filtered by heavy timber, but once on top, Lake Pend Oreille stretches out below in its entire glorious splendor.

Camping: Primitive camping opportunities exist in Auxor Basin or along the ridgeline.

Alternate Hikes: At the top, this trail, actually an old roadbed all the way up, ties in with Wellington Creek Road 489, which accesses the old Auxor Mine. This may be one of the best mountain biking trails in the Cabinets. Trail 120 crosses this old road on the ridge top and provides easy access to Round Top.

Scotchman Peaks

Perhaps the wildest, most rugged terrain in the Cabinets outside the Cabinet Mountains Wilderness is the 130,000 acres of the Scotchman Peaks. Bounded by Bull River, the Clark Fork River, and Lightning, Rattle and Keeler creeks, more than two-thirds of this portion of the West Cabinets is rugged, roadless backcountry. Only a handful of trails access this remote area, but for the most part, they are well maintained and offer some fabulous hiking experiences. Road access to various trailheads include Highway 200, Highway 56, Lightning Creek Road 419, and Road No. 473 over Rattle Pass connecting Keeler Creek and Rattle Creek between the Bull Lake Valley and Lightning Creek. The highest peak in Bonner County, Idaho, and the highest in the Idaho portion of the Cabinets is Scotchman Peak at 7,009 feet.

At the top of 6,167-foot Squaw Peak, you can discover an active forest fire lookout tower, spectacular vistas of the Clark Fork Valley and Lake Pend Oreille, and the only rock shelter in existence on the Kootenai National Forest built in 1908 by Forest Service Ranger Granville "Granny" Gordon. Five different trails access this rocky pinnacle. The lookout tower is typically manned during the summer for the purpose of spotting wildfires. Respect the privacy of the individual living there during those months.

Scotchman No. 2

Trails: Little Spar Lake, Ross Creek

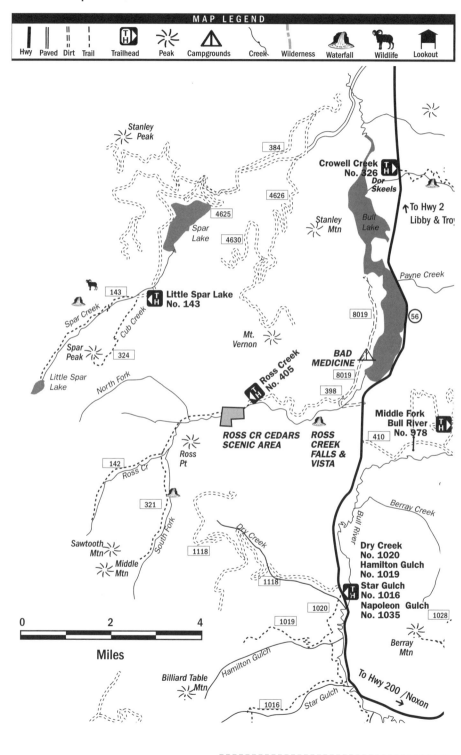

MAP LEGEND

Hwy | Paved | Dirt | Trail | Trailhead | Peak | Campgrounds | Creek | Wilderness | Waterfall | Wildlife | Lookout

Stanley Peak

384

Crowell Creek No. 326

Dor Skeels

4626

↑ To Hwy 2 Libby & Tro

4625

Spar Lake

Stanley Mtn

Bull Lake

4630

Payne Creek

143

Little Spar Lake No. 143

Cub Creek

8019

56

Spar Creek

Mt. Vernon

BAD MEDICINE

Spar Peak

324

8019

North Fork

Ross Creek No. 405

398

Little Spar Lake

Middle Fork Bull River No. 978

ROSS CR CEDARS SCENIC AREA

ROSS CREEK FALLS & VISTA

410

142

Ross Pt

Ross Cr

Berray Creek

321

South Fork

Bull River

Dry Creek

Sawtooth Mtn

1118

Dry Creek No. 1020
Hamilton Gulch No. 1019
Star Gulch No. 1016
Napoleon Gulch No. 1035

Middle Mtn

1118

1028

1020

Berray Mtn

1019

0   2   4

Miles

Hamilton Gulch

Billiard Table Mtn

To Hwy 200 / Noxon

1016

Star Gulch

Little Spar Lake Trail No. 143

Destination: Little Spar Lake. *Map, page 101.*

USGS Map: Spar Lake, Mount Pend Oreille

Trailhead: Two miles east of Troy, Montana, turn south off Highway 2 onto Lake Creek Road No. 384. Travel approximately 15 miles to Spar Lake and continue around this lake another 4 miles to the trailhead. It can also be accessed from Highway 56 by turning onto the Troy Mine Road near milepost 25 and follow the signs.

Trail Length: 4 miles one-way

Trail Condition: good

Elevation Gain: 1,800 feet

Estimated Duration of Hike: 3 to 4 hours up, 2 to 3 hours down

Sweat Index: difficult

Best Features: spectacular cliffs, alpine lake, mountain goats, waterfall

Availability of Water Along the Trail: The trail closely follows Spar Creek all the way to the lake.

Stream Crossings: a tricky one across Spar Creek about 1.5 miles up the trail, plus a couple of minor challenges across rocky side drainages

What's it like? The first mile of this trail is along an old logging road. Look for the first sign to Spar Peak, then only a couple hundred yards farther on is the sign for Little Spar Lake. The path follows one of the most scenic and dramatic stream valleys in the entire Cabinet Mountain range. Incredible cliffs line the southeast side of the creek most of the way, and it is among these cliffs that mountain goats can often be seen. At the Spar Creek stream crossing about a mile and a half up the trail, it is not unusual well into August to encounter one of the lowest elevation summertime snow banks to be found anywhere, at barely 4,000 feet. Some giant Western hemlocks are scattered along the middle portion of the trail; many of them are in excess of 12 feet in circumference. Maybe a mile and a half from the lake, the trail fords a rocky stream course above which is a beautiful waterfall, especially early in the year when runoff is high. Little Spar Lake itself is a spectacular gem with a population of small cutthroat trout.

Camping: Several primitive campsites are located near the lake.

Alternate Hikes: This trail provides great access for off-trail hiking to the summit of Scotchman No. 2 and to a small lake at the headwaters of Savage Creek. Spar Peak Trail No. 324 splits from this trail while it is still a logging road and climbs steeply to the magnificent summit of Spar Peak (6,585 feet). Trail 324 is in good condition and affords dramatic views of both the West Cabinets and the Cabinet Mountains Wilderness.

Ross Creek Nature Trail No. 405

Destination: Ross Creek Cedars. *Map, page 101.*

USGS Map: Sawtooth Mountain

Trailhead: Near milepost 17 on Highway 56 about 22 miles north of Noxon, Montana, turn west onto Ross Creek Road No. 398 (a paved, one-lane road with turnouts) and proceed 4 miles to the trailhead.

Trail Length: 1 mile one-way

Trail Condition: excellent, handicapped accessible

Elevation Gain: virtually none

Estimated Duration of Hike: 1 to 2 hours around the nature trail

Sweat Index: easy

Best Features: Some of the largest, oldest trees known in the state of Montana are here. A waterfall is located several miles above the cedar grove in the South Fork of Ross Creek.

Availability of Water Along the Trail: Ross Creek flows through the giant cedar grove.

Stream Crossings: A sturdy bridge with handrails spans the only stream.

What's it like? The Forest Service has developed a modern trailhead with toilet facilities and picnic tables and a beautiful nature trail at what is known as the Ross Creek Cedars. The trail winds through a grove of ancient cedars, some of which are more than 10 feet in diameter, or 35 feet in circumference, 200 feet tall and perhaps a thousand years old. Interpretive plaques along the wide, graveled trail enhance the visitor's experience into this cathedral forest. Lush ferns and mosses and other vegetation grow profusely in this magnificent example of a temperate rainforest. Several old snags hollowed out by fire provide a glimpse into what are called fairy dens. The trail makes a convenient loop with benches scattered along the way for meditative contemplation.

Precautions: This is a sensitive habitat preserved as a Research Natural Area. Please stay on the trail, and don't climb on the trees.

Camping: not allowed at the trailhead or in the natural area

Alternate Hikes: At the apex of the nature trail loop, Ross Creek Trail 142 continues west deep into the heart of this incredible valley. The trail forks at the confluence of the south and middle forks of the creek. Trail 142 carries on for another 2.5 miles up the middle fork, while Trail 321 goes nearly 3 miles up the south fork. A highlight of the south fork trail is a splendid waterfall a mile or so from the trail junction. You must drop below the trail a short distance to view the falls. Avid backcountry hikers use Trail 321 as an access for off-trail hiking to the summit of Sawtooth Mountain, which dominates the skyline north of Heron, Montana.

Trails: Pillick Ridge, Star Gulch, Napoleon Gulch, Big Eddy, Blacktail, Hamilton Gulch

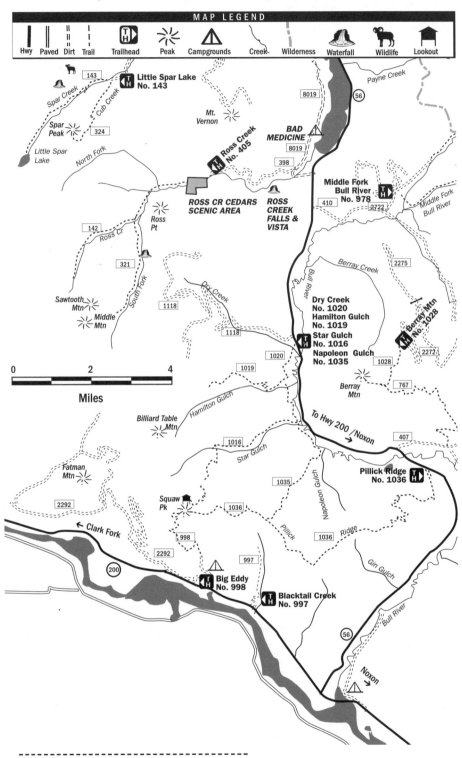

MAP LEGEND

Hwy | Paved | Dirt | Trail | Trailhead | Peak | Campgrounds | Creek | Wilderness | Waterfall | Wildlife | Lookout

143 — Little Spar Lake No. 143

Spar Creek

Cub Creek

8019

56

Payne Creek

Spar Peak

324

Mt. Vernon

BAD MEDICINE

8019

North Fork

Little Spar Lake

Ross Creek No. 405

398

Middle Fork Bull River No. 978

410

2722

Middle Fork Bull River

ROSS CR CEDARS SCENIC AREA

ROSS CREEK FALLS & VISTA

142

Ross Cr

Ross Pt

Berray Creek

2275

321

Dry Creek

1118

1118

1020

Dry Creek No. 1020
Hamilton Gulch No. 1019
Star Gulch No. 1016
Napoleon Gulch No. 1035

Bull River

Berray Mtn No. 1028

2272

Sawtooth Mtn

Middle Mtn

South Fork

1019

1028

Berray Mtn

767

0   2   4
Miles

Hamilton Gulch

To Hwy 200 / Noxon

407

Billiard Table Mtn

1016

Star Gulch

Pillick Ridge No. 1036

Fatman Mtn

1035

Napoleon Gulch

2292

Squaw Pk

1036

1036   Ridge

998

Pillick

Gin Gulch

Clark Fork

2292

997

200

Big Eddy No. 998

Blacktail Creek No. 997

Bull River

56

Noxon

Pillick Ridge No. 1036

Destination: Squaw Peak, 6,167 feet. *Map, page 104.*

USGS Map: Sawtooth Mountain, Smeads Bench

Trailhead: Near milepost 7 on Montana Highway 56 about 12 miles north of Noxon, Montana look for the trailhead sign. Turn west and go about half a mile on a narrow dirt road to the trailhead.

Trail Length: 11 miles one-way

Trail Condition: excellent

Elevation Gain: 3,400 feet

Estimated Duration of Hike: 5 to 7 hours up, 4 to 5 hours down

Sweat Index: strenuous

Best Features: unique old-growth mountain hemlock forest along parts of the crest of Pillick Ridge and excellent views of the Clark Fork and Bull River valleys

Availability of Water Along the Trail: none

Stream Crossings: none

What's it like? The Pillick Ridge trail is a horse packer's delight. Though much of the trail passes through dense forest, even along its crest, there are splendid views north, east and south from numerous vantage points along the way. High on the north-facing slope is a stunning forest comprised of ancient mountain hemlock, a high-elevation tree species found in very few places in Montana outside the Cabinets. The trail climbs rather steeply at first for several miles, then follows the undulating topography of the ridge all the way to the summit of Squaw Peak where an active forest fire lookout tower is situated.

Camping: No water along the trail means campers need to pack their own, but there are numerous places along the ridgeline that offer good primitive camping opportunities.

Alternate Hikes: Beware of an old trail junction for Napoleon Gulch about 2 miles southeast of the true junction. The real Napoleon Gulch Trail No. 1035 and Star Gulch Trail No. 1016 both join this trail atop Pillick Ridge and afford several loop hike options.

The outhouse on Squaw Peak

Star Gulch No. 1016,
Napoleon Gulch No. 1035 via Dry Creek No. 1020

Destination: Squaw Peak, 6,167 feet. *Map, page 104.*

USGS Map: Sawtooth Mountain, Smeads Bench, and Ibex Peak

Trailhead: At milepost 13 on Highway 56 about 18 miles north of Noxon, Montana, turn west on Dry Creek Road No. 1118 and find the trailhead about 100 yards from the highway on the left hand (south) side of the road. Signs placed there by the Forest Service are regularly stolen, but the path leading away into the forest is obvious.

Trail Length: Because of private property along Bull River, to access Pillick Ridge and Squaw Peak from Highway 56 via Star Gulch or Napoleon Gulch you must begin at the Dry Creek trailhead. It is about 2 miles along Trail No. 1020 to its junction with Star Gulch Trail No. 1016 and about 3.5 miles to its junction with Napoleon Gulch Trail No. 1035. Both of those trails tie in with Pillick Ridge Trail No. 1036. From Dry Creek to Squaw Peak, there are approximately 7 miles via Star Gulch and approximately 9.5 miles via Napoleon Gulch.

Trail Conditions: good to excellent

Elevation Gain: 3,300 feet

Estimated Duration of Hike: The Dry Creek-Napoleon Gulch-Star Gulch trails make for a nice, though rather long, loop hike. The total distance covers nearly 17 miles. Plan on 8 to 10 hours or more for the entire loop.

Sweat Index: strenuous

Best Features: A stunning birch forest along Star Gulch contains Montana's state champion pin cherry, pending confirmation by the Champion Tree Program. There is also a historical mining site on Star Gulch. The 360-degree views atop Squaw Peak are unmatched anywhere in the Cabinets.

Availability of Water Along the Trail: Trail No. 1035 closely follows Napoleon Gulch, a perennial stream, for a couple of miles. A spring emerges a half-mile or so below the lookout on trail No. 1016 next to a suitable camping spot and near a stunning wildflower-studded meadow. It crosses several small streams and a rather rambunctious fork of Star Gulch almost 3 miles below Squaw Peak.

Stream Crossings: Trail No. 1020 crosses Dry Creek and Hamilton Gulch, which must be waded, and Star Gulch, which has a tricky log acting as a bridge. The stream crossing on Trail No. 1016 about 2.5 miles up the trail is fraught with slick rocks and downfall.

What's it like? Trail No. 1020 is a connecting route for the trail system that accesses the southern part of the Scotchman Peaks Primitive Area. It meanders through dark cedar forests over level to gently undulating terrain. Napoleon Gulch Trail No. 1035 climbs modestly through a forest that is home to a beautiful

----

stand of grand fir towering over a forest floor carpeted in places with wild sarsa-parilla. A highlight of Star Gulch Trail No. 1016 is the unexpected birch forest that stretches for nearly a mile along the lower slopes. A remnant of early 20th centu-ry history is located high on the mountain where prospectors once built a cabin, now long gone, and dug for precious metals. In the sheltered cirque below the rocky summit of Squaw Peak are a spectacular meadow and a small gurgling spring. Views of the East Cabinets from the upper reaches of this trail are magnificent.

Camping: A small primitive campsite is located next to the spring nearly a mile below the summit of Squaw Peak.

Precautions: Following a snowy winter, drifts may obscure parts of the Star Gulch trail near the top well into the summer.

Alternate Hikes: The adventurous can bushwhack and rock hop out to Billiard Table Mountain (6,622 feet) from Squaw Peak along the ridgeline for a distance of approximately 3 miles, but it is a difficult excursion. Open loop hikes utilizing the Star Gulch, Napoleon Gulch or Big Eddy trails with Pillick Ridge make for some fine overnight excursions into this wild expanse of forest. Other bushwhack-ing opportunities can be pursued from the ends of the Blacktail Creek and Hamilton Gulch trails.

Squaw Peak Lookout

Big Eddy Trail No. 998

Destination: Squaw Peak, 6,167 feet. *Map, page 104.*

USGS Map: Heron

Trailhead: About two-tenths of a mile east of milepost 6 on Highway 200, and a little over 2 miles east of the Heron, Montana, turnoff, look for a steeply ascending, unmarked jeep trail on the north side of the highway. It is about 100 yards east of Fatman Road No. 2292. This jeep trail is blocked by a "tank trap" one-third of mile above the highway, and the turnaround area is quite small. Parking on the wide shoulder of the highway is advised.

Trail Length: Approximately 5 miles one-way

Trail Condition: excellent

Elevation Gain: 4,000 feet

Estimated Duration of Hike: 3 to 4 hours up, 2 to 3 hours down

Sweat Index: strenuous

Best Features: Access to a forest fire lookout; from the higher slopes, note the ripple marks in the fields far below left by Glacial Lake Missoula thousands of years ago.

Availability of Water Along the Trail: Big Eddy Creek is near the trail several hundred yards up from the highway, and another mile and a half along you'll find where it gushes from the mountainside in a torrential spring about 200 feet below the trail.

Stream Crossings: none

What's it like? This is one of the few trails in the entire Cabinet Mountains where you should look both ways before crossing the highway to begin your hike. The jeep track is drivable for 4WD vehicles, but only for one-third mile to the turnaround at the "tank trap." This old mining road, which hikers must follow, climbs steeply for nearly two miles. Douglas fir dominates the forest at first, and though there are occasional views of the valley, the forest cover is pretty constant almost to the top of the mountain. Lodgepole pine takes over as the most prolific tree on the higher slopes. The summit is obscured from view along most of the trail. Once you walk into the shallow swale cradling the rock shelter built in 1908 and climb the stone steps to the lookout's perch atop a rocky pinnacle, the surrounding panorama will take your breath away.

Camping: Keeping in mind there is no water on top, a great campsite is located next to the old stone building just below the lookout. Just off Highway 200 near the trailhead, Big Eddy Recreation Area offers several campsites on the Clark Fork River.

Alternate Hikes: At the top this trail connects with Star Gulch Trail No. 1016, which descends the steep, rocky east slope of Squaw Peak.

Blacktail Creek Trail No. 997

Destination: Blacktail Creek. *Map, page 104.*

USGS Map: Heron

Trailhead: Near milepost 8 on Highway 200 about 4 miles east of the Heron, Montana, turn off the highway where it crosses Blacktail Creek. A steeply ascending, power line service track leads to the trail about 150 feet off the highway on the north side. A sign marks the trail at this point. Parking is available in a turnout next to the Clark Fork River adjacent to the highway. Look both ways before crossing the road.

Trail Length: This trail dead ends after about 2 miles.

Trail Condition: good

Elevation Gain: 1,600 feet

Estimated Duration of Hike: 1 to 2 hours to the end of the trail; an hour back down

Sweat Index: moderate

Best Features: accesses what may well be a Glacial Lake Missoula terrace

Availability of Water Along the Trail: The trail lies alongside Blacktail Creek, a perennial stream, both at the beginning and end of the hike.

Stream Crossings: About a hundred yards of the trail may be under water during spring runoff near the bottom, and there is one easy crossing after about a mile.

What's it like? The trail follows the stream closely at first and passes beneath an impressive rock wall draped with mosses, lichens and other plants. Higher up it switchbacks across a steep slope, then gains a mid-elevation terrace that is likely a remnant of Glacial Lake Missoula. For almost a mile it winds farther into the forest before ending at the side of the stream.

Camping: Big Eddy Recreation Area on Highway 200 affords camping opportunities about 2 miles west of the trailhead.

Alternate Hikes: To continue to the top of Pillick Ridge from the end of this trail requires more than another mile of bushwhacking to tie in with Pillick Ridge Trail No. 1036.

Hamilton Gulch Trail No. 1019

Destination: Hamilton Gulch. *Map, page 104.*

USGS Map: Sawtooth Mountain

Trailhead: See directions for Star Gulch and Napoleon Gulch via Dry Creek, page 106.

Trail Length: 3 miles one-way to a dead end

Trail Condition: good, though deteriorating near the end

Elevation Gain: 2,000 feet

Estimated Duration of Hike: 1 to 2 hours to the end of the trail; an hour or so back down

Sweat Index: moderate

Best Features: occasional good views of Billiard Table Mountain

Availability of Water Along the Trail: From the Dry Creek trailhead, the trail closely follows Dry Creek, then crosses Hamilton Gulch just before reaching the Trail 1019 junction.

Stream Crossings: Hamilton Gulch must be waded or rock-hopped to get across and there is another easy crossing of the stream about 2.5 miles up.

What's it like? To access this trail begin at Dry Creek Trail No. 1020 and proceed for about a mile or so to this trail junction. The trail into Hamilton Gulch climbs through a young forest well above the stream and affords glimpses of the rugged spires of Billiard Table from time to time.

Camping: not really

Alternate Hikes: Some exciting, though difficult, off-trail hiking can be enjoyed beyond the end of this trail all the way to the rugged summit of Billiard Table and its satellite ridges.

Billiard Table Mountain and Hamilton Gulch as seen from the Historic Ranger Station in the East Fork Bull River

Trails: East Fork Peak, Scotchman Peak

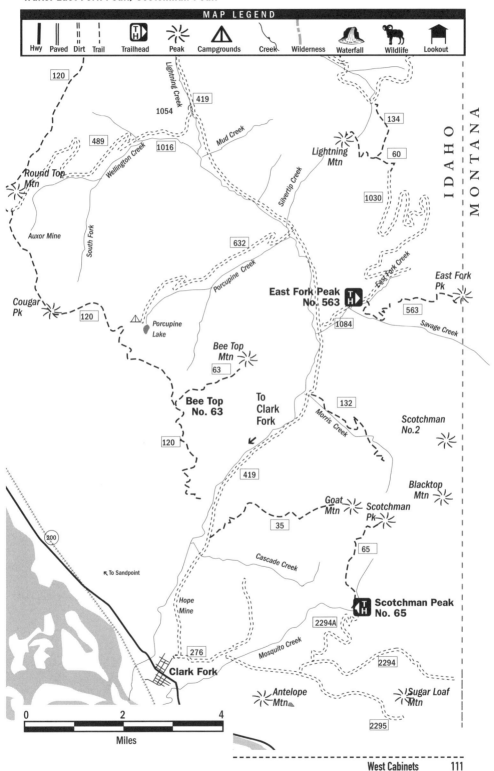

MAP LEGEND

| Hwy | Paved | Dirt | Trail | Trailhead | Peak | Campgrounds | Creek | Wilderness | Waterfall | Wildlife | Lookout |

120

Lightning Creek

419

1054

489

1016

Mud Creek

134

60

Lightning Mtn

Round Top Mtn

Wellington Creek

Silvertip Creek

1030

Auxor Mine

South Fork

632

IDAHO

MONTANA

Porcupine Creek

East Fork Creek

East Fork Pk

Cougar Pk

120

Porcupine Lake

East Fork Peak No. 563

563

1084

Savage Creek

Bee Top Mtn

63

To Clark Fork

132

Scotchman No. 2

Bee Top No. 63

120

419

Morris Creek

Blacktop Mtn

Goat Mtn

Scotchman Pk

35

200

To Sandpoint

Cascade Creek

65

Hope Mine

Scotchman Peak No. 65

2294A

276

Clark Fork

Mosquito Creek

2294

Antelope Mtn

Sugar Loaf Mtn

2295

0   2   4

Miles

Scotchman Peak Trail No. 65

Destination: Scotchman Peak, 7,009 feet. *Map, page 111.*

USGS Map: Clark Fork

Trailhead: In downtown Clark Fork, Idaho, turn north by the Chevron Station, go past the school and continue up Mosquito Creek Road 276 past the Clark Fork Field Campus to the junction of Road No. 2294; take a right and go 1.2 miles to Road 2294A, then left for another 1.2 miles to the trailhead.

Trail Length: 4 miles one-way

Trail Condition: good

Elevation Gain: 3,700 feet

Estimated Duration of Hike: 3 to 4 hours up, 2 to 3 hours down

Sweat Index: strenuous

Best Features: spectacular views of Lake Pend Oreille and the West Cabinets

Availability of Water Along the Trail: minimal trickles in a few seepy areas

Stream Crossings: none

This lookout on Scotchman Peak, now gone, once looked out over the town of Clark Fork, Idaho.

What's it like? This steep trail passes through a variety of forest types and a wonderful subalpine meadow on its way to the highest peak in Bonner County and the highest peak in the Idaho portion of the Cabinets. The jagged summit of Scotchman Peak is a jumble of rocks at 7,009 feet. A lookout tower once sat upon this peak. It has been removed, but some evidence remains. A large wildfire burned to the ridge top in 1994, and the effects of that are seen close up within a mile of the summit. The views from along this trail are magnificent, especially as the hiker gains elevation and the expanse of Lake Pend Oreille dominates the vista to the southwest. From the peak, the rugged nature of the proposed Scotchman Peaks Wilderness to the north is obvious, and the panorama of the high country of the Cabinet Mountains Wilderness to the east is awesome. You don't want to miss the most fascinating feature of this hike – the hundreds of pieces of rock art that hikers have built near the summit over the years. It is an incredible gallery of unique art.

Camping: not really

Alternate Hikes: Several other trails access the west side of the Scotchmans from Lightning Creek, but maintenance is poor and these trails dead end. Still, for an excursion into some fabulous backcountry, they provide an interesting avenue. Look for the trailheads along Lightning Creek Road No. 419 for Goat Mountain Trail No. 35, Regal Creek Trail No. 556 and Morris Creek Trail No. 132.

East Fork Peak Trail No. 563

Destination: East Fork Peak, 5,987 feet. *Map, page 111.*

Trailhead: Finding this trailhead is a challenge since it is not clearly marked. Take Trestle Creek Road No. 275 from Highway 200 between Pack River and Hope, Idaho, to Lightning Creek Road No. 419. Follow Lightning Creek Road No. 419 approximately 10 miles, then turn east onto East Fork Creek Road No. 1084 and proceed 0.9 mile to a narrow track leading south toward the creek. A well-used campsite is located here with a log crossing to the south side of the creek. It is best to simply cut straight uphill once across the stream for approxi-

Jill Davies on top of East Fork Peak

mately 150 vertical feet until you come upon an old logging road now maintained as the trail. Less than a mile along this easy stroll, the trail to East Fork Peak takes an obvious turn to the left uphill. You can also get to this trailhead by taking Lightning Creek Road No. 419 out of Clark Fork, but about 6 miles up the road has been washed out where it crosses East Fork Creek and only 4WD vehicles can make it across at times of low water.

Trail Length: 3 miles one-way

Trail Condition: fair to good

Elevation Gain: 3,200 feet

Estimated Duration of Hike: 2 to 3 hours up, 1 to 2 hours down

Sweat Index: strenuous

Best Features: excellent views of several of the high peaks in the West Cabinets

Availability of Water Along the Trail: Once across East Fork Creek at the bottom, there is no water along this trail.

Stream Crossings: A log crosses East Fork Creek adjacent to the campsite just off Road No. 1084, but it is tricky to negotiate.

What's it like? East Fork Peak is only 5,987 feet in elevation, but what a superb view from its rocky turrets. Savage Mountain looms high to the southeast and Scotchman No. 2 dominates the horizon across Savage Creek to the south.

To the north are grand vistas of Char Creek, Thunder Creek (and the results of a forest fire in 2000), Drift Peak, Twin Peaks and Lightning Mountain. The trail passes through a forest dominated by Douglas fir, some of which is large old-growth timber. Alpine larch is commonplace in the high country of the Cabinets, but rarely is it ever found below 6,500 or even 7,000 feet – East Fork Peak is one of the only places I know with this high-elevation tree occurring under 6,000 feet. One of the more interesting botanical features along the trail is the off-site presence of devil's club high on a dry south slope, when normally it is found in low elevation, moist cedar bottoms. A short ways east of the highest point on this rocky summit is a steel marker identifying the Montana-Idaho state line.

Precautions: Outfitters do most of the maintenance on this trail, though the Forest Service checks it out every few years. It is easy to follow, once the trail is located after crossing the creek.

Camping: A primitive campsite is located at the trailhead.

Alternate Hikes: Savage Creek Trail No. 61 continues along the old logging road where the East Fork Peak trail begins to switchback up the mountainside, but it is overgrown, poorly maintained and difficult to follow. It stays on the logging road up through an old remote clear-cut, then becomes a trail to a rocky ridge about a mile northwest of Scotchman No. 2. From the top of East Fork Peak, it is possible to ascend Savage Mountain (6,906 feet).

Origins

A sudden clattering of rocks on the cliffs and the echo of hooves on their crumbling sedimentary layers gave away the presence of mountain goats. Impossibly, they climbed a face of stone so steep that not even trees could maintain a foothold. But with unassuming ease they leapt from ledge to ledge until they were out of sight and a safe distance from the man who had disrupted the solitude of their alpine sanctuary.

I did not see the goats, but Mike did. He had gone to fetch water for breakfast while Sandy and I muddled around the campsite we had spied the day before from across the canyon.

The saddle between the West Fork of Blue Creek and the Middle Fork of Ross Creek was where we wanted to spend the night, but it was no easy task getting there. We had done well hiking the rugged terrain above Little Spar Lake, but we weren't mountain goats and our packs were heavy. The broken rock, the narrow ridges, the tangled forest, the sharply rising mountainsides had all contributed to our fatigue, yet by the end of the day, three of the five that had started out on this adventure made it to 48 Hour Pass.

Don't worry, the other two didn't fall off a cliff or get eaten by a mountain lion. We had all climbed from a sedgy meadow – the site of our first night's camp – to the top of a glaciated divide, then four of us carried on to the summit of Scotchman No. 2, the sibling of Clark Fork's more famous mountaintop, Scotchman Peak. A mere 20 feet less in height, No. 2 is absolutely no less spectacular. Connected by the fractured black and gray sedimentary rock of Black Top Mountain, these three peaks form a jagged wall of untamed rugged beauty.

When the four of us returned to where we had left our packs and where Renee enjoyed the meditative silence of the high country, we ate lunch and studied the route that

Bighorn sheep on Berray Mountain

would take us to the pass. Renee and David decided to return to the splendid meadow in which we had become coated in frost the cold August night before. From there they dropped back to the shores of Little Spar Lake and camped by its placid, reflective surface, reflecting in their own ways upon the serenity of the wilderness of the Scotchman Peaks.

Sandy, Mike and I continued along the headwall encircling Little Spar Lake to a high point where we turned south toward the pass. Before us lay the jumbled mass of The Compton Crags, so named by another avid backcountry explorer, Kevin Davis, for one of the families who have long lived at the mouth of Blue Creek. Nan Compton is still there and Sandy, being the oldest of the three Compton boys, was along on this hike, interested in exploring his origins.

He explained, while we traipsed among the stony highlands of the Scotchmans, that Native American clans in southern Idaho developed their identities by the watersheds in which they lived. They became known by the totality of their ancestors and families as well as by the streams and mountains and forests of their home territories. In like fashion, Sandy wanted to discover the nature of his home watershed, Blue Creek, and find its origin among the peaks he has long admired and long explored. But it is a big world in the primitive backcountry of the West Cabinets, and for the first time he was about to meet the birthplace of the West Fork of Blue Creek.

At about 5,000 feet in elevation, the west fork makes a fishhook turn, if you are going upstream, away from the slabs of rock protruding from the flanks of Scotchman No. 2. The ascent out of the canyon toward the bedrock thrust nearly a mile above the valley floor is a precipitous one. At the top of the ascent an amphitheater carved deep into the mountainside harbors the remains of what could well be an ancient glacier. It is here that water trickles from beneath a glacial moraine and down the flat surface of a luminescent rock not a hundred feet from the snow and ice feeding it.

Sandy searched the moraine, the cauldron of rock fashioned by ice and snow and water over eons of patient masonry, exploring this point of origin and connecting it to his own origins in the valley far below.

I fell to my knees, leaned forward and drank tentatively from the icy brook. The waters sang in the chilled thin air as it made its very first contact with the earth and sky. For so long it had been bound up in ice, frozen until the sun could free it to cascade from one rocky cairn to another in a rambunctious run to the big river miles away.

The virility of youth surged through me; vivacious Life as new as the snowmelt, as fresh as the flowers blooming at the water's edge. And for one fleeting moment, I tasted the age of the rock, the antiquity of the mountains, and a simple truth dawned inside me: Youth and age are inseparable where all things begin.

Section III:

The Southern Cabinets

The Lay of the Land

The southern end of the Cabinet Mountains is likely the least-known part of an already little-known range of mountains. Many locals in northwest Montana are familiar with Vermilion River, Thompson River and the Cube Iron-Silcox primitive area – also known as the Cabinet Lakes Country – but few of the inhabitants in the surrounding communities and even fewer outsiders know about the fabulous hiking to be had here.

This part of the Cabinets is also the most confusing when it comes to land ownership. No more than half of it is public land; almost half belongs to giant timber corporations. There are also State and private holdings scattered across the landscape. This does not include the far southeastern portion of the range, bounded by the Little Bitterroot River, the Flathead River and the Reservation Divide from Teepee Mountain to Knowles Creek. The far southeast portion of the range is on the Flathead Indian Reservation.

Public lands here are managed by the Kootenai and Lolo national forests. Between these two agencies and corporate timber interests, a vast network of

Winter camping on Twenty Peak overlooking the Clark Fork River

roads has been developed over the past 50 years. Primary access points are in the Vermilion River, both ends of the Thompson River, Silver Butte and McGinnis Meadows. There are others, too, and they are all interconnected.

The communities adjacent to the public's portion of the southern Cabinets include Trout Creek, Thompson Falls, Plains and Paradise, Montana. On the reservation there are also Dixon, Hot Springs, Lonepine and Niarada, Montana. The northeast side of this section is characterized by a long stretch of Highway 2 from Libby to McGregor Lake where the most civilized hamlet may well be Happy's Inn.

Despite the decades of unrestrained timber harvest across much of this terrain, some small and large pockets of wild country remain. Between Galena Creek, Allen Peak, Cataract Peak, Sundance Ridge, Baldy and Cube Iron-Silcox, there are 150,000 acres, or more than 230 square miles, from the south end of the CMW to Rainbow Lake that offer primitive or wilderness-like experiences for the hiker.

Among these wildlands are seven named peaks over 7,000 feet and more than two-dozen lakes, not including the Thompson Chain of Lakes bordering the northeast corner. The only National Recreation Trail to be found in the Cabinets is located on Baldy Mountain (7,464 feet) north of Plains. It is the highest peak in the Cabinets outside the wilderness. Other popular hikes include the myriads of trails in the Cabinet Lakes Country, best accessed from the West Fork Thompson River, and a system of trails in the Vermilion to places like Seven Point Mountain (6,660 feet), Canyon Peak (6,326 feet) and Allen Peak (6,740 feet) on the Vermilion-Silver Butte Divide.

Numerous small lakes fill low- and high-elevation basins here, from Elk Lake at 4,200 feet to Baldy Lake at over 6,700 feet. Between them are more than 20 other lakes, many of them supporting populations of different kinds of trout. The Cabinets' largest interior river system is located in the south end, the Thompson River, and two of the most scenic waterfalls anywhere in the range are here, Vermilion Falls and Graves Creek Falls.

The forgotten corner of the Cabinets – the southern corner – offers some excellent hiking opportunities easily accessible from the region's two main highways. Just a little bit of research may turn up some of the best destinations that can be reached by foot, horseback or mountain bike.

Vermilion-Fisher River

Just south of the Cabinet Mountains Wilderness is a block of public land bounded by Swamp Creek, the Vermilion River and Silver Butte Pass encompassing more than 20,000 acres. Adjacent to it is another 30,000 acres sprawling between the Vermilion River and Graves Creek. And east and north of those two wild areas are yet another 25,000 acres wrapped around Allen Peak, all of which have never been developed.

The only thing separating these wildlands from the wilderness is a power line and the access road utilized for its maintenance. A few other roads provide access to this primitive backcountry, including Vermilion River Road No. 154, Graves Creek Road No. 367 and Silver Butte Fisher River Road No. 148. It is these vast expanses of de facto wilderness that link the CMW to the proposed Cube Iron-Silcox Wilderness north of Thompson Falls.

A unique aspect of this Vermilion-Fisher River country is that it is heavily timbered but has experienced minimal incursion from logging operations, excluding the upper Vermilion River. This means these 75,000 acres offer some fantastic forest hiking. The best access is from Highway 200 in Montana at Trout Creek or Thompson Falls or Highway 2 about 20 miles south of Libby, Montana.

From Twenty Peak looking north across Galena Creek to the CMW

Trails: 20-Odd Peak, Canyon Peak

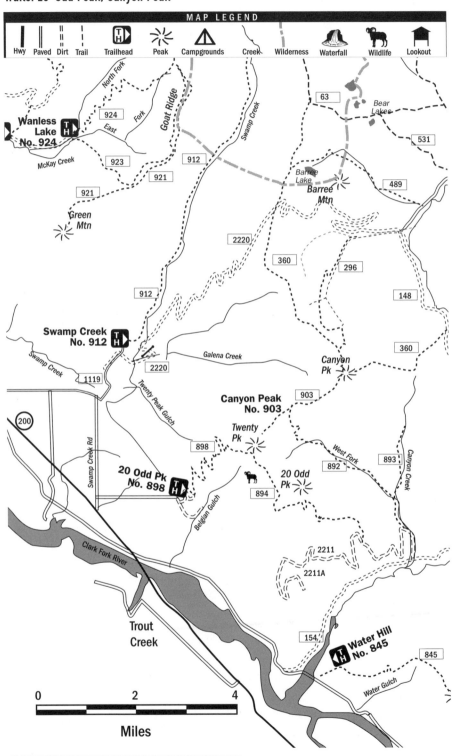

MAP LEGEND

Hwy | Paved | Dirt | Trail | Trailhead | Peak | Campgrounds | Creek | Wilderness | Waterfall | Wildlife | Lookout

North Fork

East Fork

Goat Ridge

Swamp Creek

63

Bear Lakes

924

Wanless Lake No. 924

531

McKay Creek

923

912

921

Barree Lake

489

921

Barree Mtn

Green Mtn

2220

360

296

912

148

Swamp Creek No. 912

Galena Creek

360

Swamp Creek

2220

Canyon Pk

1119

Twenty Peak Gulch

Canyon Peak No. 903

903

Twenty Pk

200

Swamp Creek Rd

898

West Fork

893

20 Odd Pk No. 898

892

20 Odd Pk

894

Belgian Gulch

Clark Fork River

Canyon Creek

2211

2211A

Trout Creek

154

Water Hill No. 845

845

Water Gulch

0   2   4

Miles

20 Odd Peak Trail No. 898

Destination: Twenty Peak, 6,171 feet, and 20 Odd Peak, 6,049 feet. *Map, page 120.*

USGS Map: Trout Creek

Trailhead: Between mileposts 26 and 27 on Highway 200 in Montana, turn north onto Swamp Creek Road. Go one-quarter mile and take a right and proceed just over a mile and a half to the trailhead. The trailhead is located on county property next to a gravel pit.

Trail Length: 5.5 miles one-way

Trail Condition: good

Estimated Duration of Hike: 3 to 4 hours up, 2 to 3 hours down

Sweat Index: strenuous

Best Features: great views of the Clark Fork Valley, wildlife viewing including deer and elk

View from Twenty Peak of the Clark Fork Valley

Availability of Water Along the Trail: none

Stream Crossings: none

What's it like? Twenty Peak and 20 Odd Peak create a dramatically scenic backdrop for the community of Trout Creek, Montana, north of the Clark Fork River. The vast brush fields and meadows cloaking these two mountains, interspersed with ravines and draws full of timber, present some of the best wildlife habitat in the lower Clark Fork Valley. The trail begins on county property and climbs through one of these brush fields, then enters a stand of young lodgepole pine and larch. Nearly 2 miles up it comes out onto a rocky pinnacle overlooking Belgian Gulch and the valley. From there, the trail switchbacks through a forest of almost pure lodgepole pine before cutting across a steep, open slope to the site where an old lookout once sat atop 20 Odd Peak. Fabulous grassy meadows are draped on both sides of the ridge connecting these two peaks. Views of the high wilderness peaks to the north are especially good from Twenty Peak, but the real treat is the awesome perspective of the Clark Fork Valley all the way from Thompson Falls to Lake Pend Oreille, which can be seen from up on top.

Camping: Though water is not available, there are some good ridge-top camping opportunities here.

Alternate Hikes: This trail ties in with Canyon Peak Trail No. 903 and Roe Gulch Trail No. 894 at the site of the old lookout on 20 Odd.

Canyon Peak Trail No. 903

Destination: Twenty Peak, 6,171 feet, Canyon Peak, 6,326 feet. *Map, page 120.*

USGS Map: Trout Creek

Trailhead: This is a connecting trail between 20 Odd Peak Trail 898 and Cabinet Divide Trail 360. Follow directions to the trailhead for 20 Odd Peak Trail No. 898, page 121.

Trail Length: 3.5 miles one-way

Trail Condition: good

Elevation Gain: 300 feet

Estimated Duration of Hike: 1 to 2 hours either way

Sweat Index: moderate

Best Features: excellent ridge-top hiking, views of the Cabinets in all directions

Availability of Water Along the Trail: none

Stream Crossings: none

What's it like? Hiking this trail is more like strolling through a park. Other than for a short duration through mountain hemlock on the steep northeast flank of Twenty Peak, this is a true ridgeline trail. Much of the ridge is forested, but the trees are stunted, and enough openings occur to allow for gazing into Galena Creek on the north and Canyon Creek on the south.

Camping: The scarcity of water means packing plenty if you plan to camp along this ridge, which offers some great primitive overnight opportunities.

Alternate Hikes: This trail provides the means to get from 20 Odd Peak to Canyon Peak on the Cabinet Divide, which then affords opportunities to hike into the CMW or to Silver Butte Pass and access to the Allen Peak primitive area. West Fork Canyon Creek Trail 892 joins this trail about halfway between Twenty Peak and Canyon Peak.

Trails: Allen Peak, Moose Peak, Elk Lake, Elk Mountain

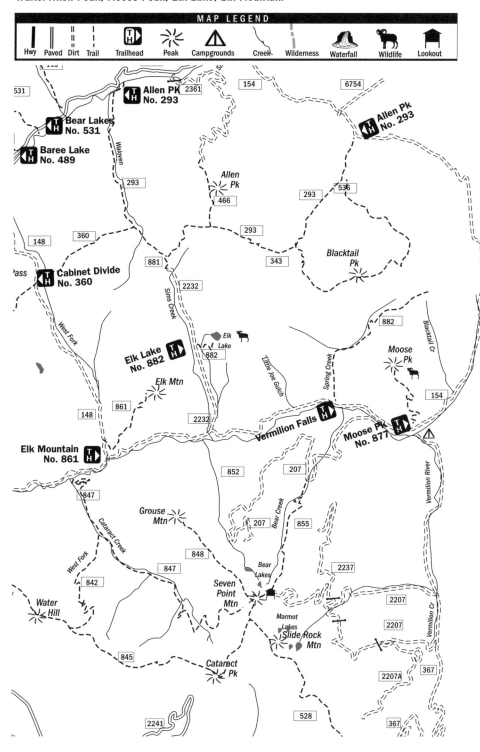

MAP LEGEND

| Hwy | Paved | Dirt | Trail | Trailhead | Peak | Campgrounds | Creek | Wilderness | Waterfall | Wildlife | Lookout |

531

154   6754

Allen Pk No. 293   2361

Bear Lakes No. 531

Baree Lake No. 489

Allen Pk No. 293

Waloven

293

Allen Pk   466

293   536

148   360

881   293   343

Blacktail Pk

Pass

Cabinet Divide No. 360

2232

Sims Creek

882   Blacktail Cr

Elk Lake   882

Elk Lake No. 882

Little Joe Gulch

Spring Creek

Moose Pk

West Fork

Elk Mtn

154

148   861

2232   Vermilion Falls   Moose Pk No. 877

Elk Mountain No. 861

852   207

847   Grouse Mtn

207   855   Bear Creek

Vermilion River

848

West Fork   847

Bear Lakes   2237

842   2207

Water Hill   Cataract Creek   Seven Point Mtn   2207

Marmot Lakes   Slide Rock Mtn

845   Cataract Pk   2207A   367

2241   528   367

Allen Peak Trail No. 293 via Trail Nos. 881 and 466

Destination: Allen Peak, 6,740 feet. *Map, page 123.*

USGS Map: Silver Butte Pass, Miller Lake

Trailhead: To get to Allen Peak, turn onto the Blue Slide Road from Highway 200 at milepost 28 about 2 miles west of Trout Creek, Montana. Follow that road 4 miles to the junction of Vermilion River Road 154 and follow it to milepost 10 and the junction of Sims Creek Road 2232. Turn north and go about 5 miles to the end of this rough road and the trailhead for Trail 881. That trail connects to Trail 293 and 466 to Allen Peak.

Trail Length: 2.5 miles one-way

Trail Conditions: good

Elevation Gain: 2,500 feet

Estimated Duration of Hike: 1 to 2 hours up, 1 to 1.5 hours down

Sweat Index: moderate

Best Features: tremendous views of the Cabinet Mountains in all directions

Allen Peak as seen from Cabinet Divide

Availability of Water Along the Trail: might find a trickle in Sims Creek near the trailhead

Stream Crossings: one minor crossing

What's it like? The ridges and peaks between the Vermilion River, Silver Butte Fisher River and East Fisher Creek are heavily forested but largely undisturbed. The views from the upper slopes and ridge tops of this unbroken forest are impressive. The hike from Sims Creek to Allen Peak is relatively easy, though the rate of elevation gain is a thousand feet every mile. Once on top, however, the vistas are splendid, and the summit of Allen Peak makes for a great place for a picnic.

Camping: a primitive campsite is located at the trailhead in Sims Creek.

Alternate Hikes: A good interconnecting trail system encompasses Allen Peak and the surrounding countryside. Trail 293 actually begins and ends in the Silver Butte Fisher River drainage and covers a total of about 12 miles. It traverses Waloven Creek and Himes Creek by going over Allen Peak. Trail 466 begins as a gated road, No. 2361, on Silver Butte Road 148 and accesses an electronic site in about 4 miles. The last mile to the peak is single-track trail, and on the south side of the peak it connects to Trail 293. Trail 360 connects to 293 in Waloven Creek, and Trails 536 and 343 split off from Trail 293 in Himes Creek.

Moose Peak Trail No. 877

Destination: Moose Peak, 6,010 feet. *Map, page 123.*

USGS Map: Miller Lake

Trailhead: At milepost 28 on Highway 200 about 2 miles west of Trout Creek, Montana, turn onto the Blue Slide Road and follow it 4 miles to Vermilion River Road No. 154. The trailhead is at milepost 13 on Vermilion River Road No. 154.

Trail Length: 3 miles one-way

Trail Condition: fair to good (obscure tread and brush clogs the last mile)

Elevation Gain: 2,400 feet

Estimated Duration of Hike: 2 to 3 hours up, 1 to 2 hours down

Sweat Index: moderate

Best Features: wildlife viewing, especially deer, elk and moose; great mountain views

Availability of Water Along the Trail: none

Stream Crossings: none

What's it like? The lower half of this trail switchbacks through vast open brush fields and, for a ways, follows a ridge that offers some good views across these brush fields, which are prime habitat for wildlife. As the trail climbs, notice advanced stages of diseases and insect infestations affecting the health of the forest; there are lots of dead Douglas fir and lodgepole pine here. The top is a rocky summit that provides great views of the upper Vermilion and the expansive forests of the Allen Peak primitive area. A lookout was once located here.

Camping: A remote Forest Service campground at Willow Creek is less than a half-mile from this trailhead.

Alternate Hikes: Some good off-trail hiking can connect with Spring Creek Trail 878 and Blacktail Peak Trail 536.

Elk Lake Trail No. 882

Destination: Elk Lake. *Map, page 123.*

USGS Map: Silver Butte Pass, Seven Point Mountain

Trailhead: At milepost 28 on Highway 200 about 2 miles west of Trout Creek, Montana, turn onto the Blue Slide Road and follow it 4 miles to Vermilion River Road No. 154. At milepost 10 on Vermilion River Road No. 154 take Sims Creek Road 2232 approximately 3 miles to the trailhead.

Trail Length: 1 mile one-way

Trail Condition: good

Elevation Gain: 500 feet

Estimated Duration of Hike: 1 hour up, 1 hour down

Sweat Index: moderate

Best Features: pristine forest lake, wildlife viewing

Availability of Water Along the Trail: A couple of small streams offer water along the bottom of the trail.

Stream Crossings: two easy crossings

What's it like? This short, moderately steep hike accesses a nice lake surrounded by thick forest. Though there are fish in the lake, it is hard-hit by fishermen because access is easy. The forest crowds the shoreline, making access to the water a bit tricky. But it is a pretty setting and makes a good destination for a picnic. It is not unusual to see moose in this vicinity.

Camping: Primitive camping is possible near the lake.

Some fine fish come from the Cabinets, such as this rainbow trout caught and released by Chris Richardson.

Elk Mountain Trail No. 861

Destination: Elk Mountain, 5,673 feet. *Map, page 123.*

USGS Map: Seven Point Mountain, Silver Butte Pass

Trailhead: At milepost 28 on Highway 200 about 2 miles west of Trout Creek, Montana, turn onto the Blue Slide Road and follow it 4 miles to Vermilion River Road No. 154. Near milepost 7 on Vermilion River Road 154, turn north onto Silver Butte Pass Road 148 and go about 1.5 miles to the signed trailhead.

Trail Length: 3.5 miles one-way

Trail Condition: fair to good

Elevation Gain: 2,500 feet

Estimated Duration of Hike: 2 to 3 hours up, 2 to 3 hours down

Sweat Index: difficult

Best Features: mountain views

Availability of Water Along the Trail: none

Stream Crossings: none

What's it like? This trail begins at the edge of a terrace left by a Glacial Lake Missoula in Lyons Gulch, a timber-harvest area, and pushes up a gentle slope to the ridgeline. From here 2 miles of steep switchbacks takes the hiker higher onto this rugged ridge. A lookout tower once sat on Elk Mountain, but it has long since been dismantled. The rocky summit offers great views all the way from Vermilion Bay to Vermilion Falls.

Camping: not really

Alternate Hikes: Some fine ridgeline hiking can be enjoyed off-trail all the way to Allen Peak.

Trails: Cataract Creek, Water Hill

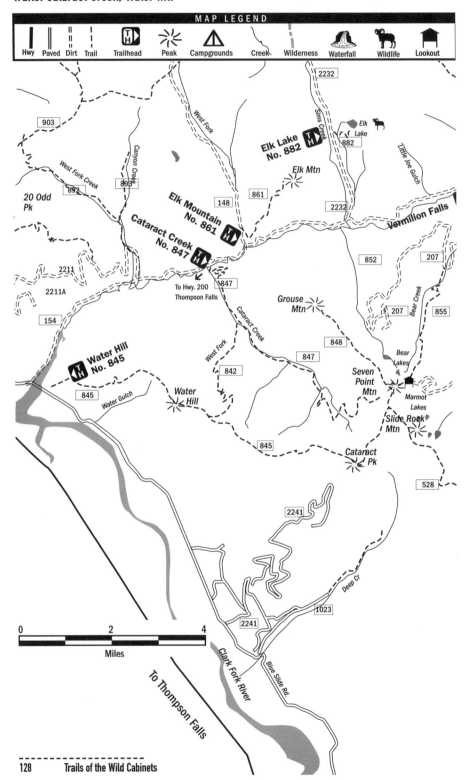

MAP LEGEND

Hwy | Paved | Dirt | Trail | Trailhead | Peak | Campgrounds | Creek | Wilderness | Waterfall | Wildlife | Lookout

2232

903

West Fork

Sims Creek

Elk Lake

Elk Lake
No. 882

Little Joe Gulch

West Fork Creek

Canyon Creek

893

893

Elk Mtn

882

20 Odd
Pk

Elk Mountain
No. 861

148

861

2232

Vermillion Falls

Cataract Creek
No. 847

852

207

2211

2211A

847

To Hwy. 200
Thompson Falls

847

Grouse
Mtn

207

855

154

Cataract Creek

Bear Creek

West Fork

848

847

Bear
Lakes

Water Hill
No. 845

842

Seven
Point
Mtn

845

Water Gulch

Water
Hill

Marmot
Lakes

Slide Rock
Mtn

845

Cataract
Pk

528

2241

Deep Cr

1023

2241

0   2   4

Miles

Clark Fork River

Blue Slide Rd.

To Thompson Falls

Cataract Creek Trail No. 847

Destination: Seven Point Mountain, 6,660 feet. *Map, page 128.*

USGS Map: Seven Point Mountain

Trailhead: At milepost 28 on Highway 200 about 2 miles west of Trout Creek, Montana, turn onto the Blue Slide Road and follow it 4 miles to Vermilion River Road No. 154. At milepost 5 on Vermilion River Road 154, find the signed trailhead.

Trail Length: 7.5 miles one-way

Trail Condition: good

Elevation Gain: 3,900 feet

Estimated Duration of Hike: 4 to 5 hours up, 3 to 4 hours down

Sweat Index: strenuous

Best Features: Glacial Lake Missoula terrace, fantastic views from on top, old forest fire lookout tower

Availability of Water Along the Trail: The trail closely follows Cataract Creek for several miles and crosses the stream a number of times.

Stream Crossings: Once across the Vermilion River, which must be waded and is about thigh-deep in late summer, there are four more small stream crossings.

What's it like? The Vermilion River is a cold mountain stream that flows fast. An extra pair of shoes is recommended for wading. Once across, the trail climbs swiftly up 500 vertical feet to the beginning of an ancient Glacial Lake Missoula terrace and follows this feature for 2 miles. Most of this country was burned in 1910, so the forest is relatively young, though a few old cedars remain near the stream. About 5.5 miles up the trail, notice a rocky knob maybe a hundred yards off trail. It is worth the short bushwhack to enjoy a fine view of the entire Cataract Creek drainage. At the top of Seven Point Mountain, the view is spectacular of nearby lakes and distant high peaks. The remains of a lookout tower are here, and an effort is afoot to rebuild it.

Camping: Several places along the stream can be utilized for primitive campsites, while the top of the mountain makes for a great overnight destination. Water is within about 30 minutes of the summit by taking an old trail down the southeast slope of Seven Point to one of the nearby Marmot Lakes. A primitive campsite is located at the trailhead.

Alternate Hikes: West Fork Cataract Creek Trail 842 splits off from this trail about 2 miles from the trailhead and climbs Water Hill where it connects with Trail 845. About a mile below the summit, Grouse Mountain Trail 848 forks from this trail. At Seven Point Mountain, this trail connects with Bear Creek Trail 855 and Vermilion-Seven Point Trail 528.

Water Hill Trail No. 845

Destination: Water Hill, 6,111 feet, and Cataract Peak, 6,205 feet. *Map, page 128.*

USGS Map: Seven Point Mountain

Trailhead: Turn east off Highway 200 at milepost 28 about 2 miles west of Trout Creek, Montana, onto the Blue Slide Road and follow it 4 miles to Vermilion Bay. The trailhead is on the east side of the bay and is marked with a sign.

Trail Length: 12 miles one-way (if taken all the way to its junction with Trail No. 528 near Seven Point Mountain).

Trail Condition: poor to fair

Elevation Gain: 4,000 feet (3,800 feet in the first 4 miles)

Estimated Duration of Hike: 6 to 8 hours up, 4 to 6 hours down

Sweat Index: strenuous

Best Features: great views of the Clark Fork Valley, good ridgeline hiking once you get up on the ridge

Availability of Water Along the Trail: Don't let the name of this geographic feature fool you – there is no water along this trail.

Stream Crossings: none

What's it like? The start of this trail is easy to find and could not be in a prettier spot, next to Vermilion Bay. It skirts private property for the first half-mile, then continues climbing rather steeply, switchbacking up a ridge until the tread is essentially lost. But by staying on the main ridgeline and persevering, the trail can be found once again – and maybe lost again, perhaps several times – until nearing the top of Water Hill. From here the trail is easier to follow since it stays on the ridge all the way to Cataract Peak. The sometimes dense, sometimes scattered forests on these mountains are interspersed with fine meadows and rocky openings that allow incredible views of the Clark Fork River Valley to the south and west and the wilds of Cataract Creek to the north.

Camping: Water is hard, if not impossible, to find along this hike, but by packing plenty, some great camping can be enjoyed along this ridge system.

Precautions: Portions of this trail are difficult to follow, especially a couple of miles from the trailhead at Vermilion Bay.

Alternate Hikes: Trail 842 rises out of the West Fork of Cataract Creek and joins this trail a mile or so west of the summit of Water Hill. The east end of this trail connects with Vermilion Pass Trail 528 near Seven Point Mountain.

Trails: Vermilion-Seven Point, Vermilion Falls

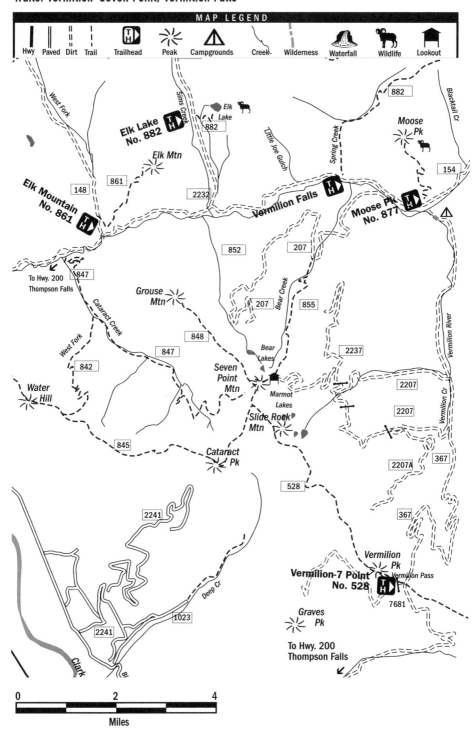

MAP LEGEND

Hwy | Paved | Dirt | Trail | Trailhead | Peak | Campgrounds | Creek | Wilderness | Waterfall | Wildlife | Lookout

West Fork

882

Blacktail Cr

Elk Lake
No. 882

Sims Creek

Elk
Lake

882

Little Joe Gulch

Spring Creek

Moose
Pk

154

Elk Mtn

148

861

2232

Vermilion Falls

Moose Pk
No. 877

Elk Mountain
No. 861

To Hwy. 200
Thompson Falls

847

852

207

Cataract Creek

Grouse
Mtn

207

Bear Creek

855

West Fork

848

847

842

Bear
Lakes

2237

Vermilion River

Water
Hill

Seven
Point
Mtn

Marmot
Lakes

2207

2207

Slide Rock
Mtn

Vermilion Cr

845

Cataract
Pk

2207A

367

528

367

2241

Deep Cr

Vermilion
Pk

Vermilion-7 Point
No. 528

Vermilion Pass

1023

7681

2241

Graves
Pk

Clark

To Hwy. 200
Thompson Falls

0   2   4

Miles

Vermilion-Seven Point Trail No. 528

Destination: Vermilion Peak, 6,700 feet; Seven Point Mountain, 6,660 feet. *Map, page 131.*

USGS Map: Vermilion Peak

Trailhead: A mile west of Thompson Falls, Montana, turn north off Highway 200 onto the Blue Slide Road. Follow it about 7 miles to Graves Creek Road No. 367 and go 10.5 miles to Vermilion Pass. The trail is less than 100 feet behind a locked gate on a spur road that goes west.

Trail Length: 6 miles one-way

Trail Condition: fair to good

Elevation Gain: 600 feet

Estimated Duration of Hike: 1 hour to Vermilion Peak, 3 to 4 hours to Seven Point Mountain, 3 to 4 hours back

Sweat Index: difficult

Best Features: terrific mountain views, spectacular waterfall on the way to the trailhead, old lookout tower

Availability of Water Along the Trail: none

Stream Crossings: none

What's it like? This easy hike is made more difficult only because of the distance it covers. From the pass, the trail climbs easily to a fine meadow and views of Graves Creek and the rugged ridges of the Cube Iron-Silcox proposed wilderness. Those views are vastly improved by taking a short spur trail to the top of Vermilion Peak (6,700 feet) only a mile or so from the trailhead. Once around Vermilion Peak, Trail 528 meanders lazily along the ridgeline through a dense forest until finally breaking out into talus rock at the head end of Deep Creek on the backside of Slide Rock Mountain. The views are excellent and continue likewise all the way to Seven Point. These higher ridges are characterized by pristine meadows with scattered, stunted trees; just over their edges in several small basins below the peak are a variety of lakes, including Marmot Lakes, Bear Lake and Grouse Lake. The old Seven Point lookout has been mostly dismantled, but an effort is under way to rebuild and restore it since it was listed on the Register of National Historic Places.

Camping: Good camping can be found all along the ridge, especially near the summit of Seven Point Mountain, and additional great camping opportunities can be found at any of the lakes below it.

Alternate Hikes: On the way up Graves Creek Road No. 367 to Vermilion Pass, you can stop to view Graves Creek Falls at about the 3-mile marker. On the ridge between Slide Rock Mountain and Seven Point, Water Hill Trail 845 connects with Trail 528 less than a mile from the lookout. This trail also connects to Trail Nos. 847 and 855, providing for some terrific open loops through this serene backcountry.

Vermilion Falls Trail (no designated trail number)

Destination: Vermilion Falls. *Map, page 131.*

USGS Map: Seven Point Mountain, Vermilion Peak

Trailhead: At milepost 28 on Highway 200 about 2 miles west of Trout Creek, Montana, turn onto the Blue Slide Road and follow it 4 miles to Vermilion River Road No. 154. Find the sign and a turnout for the falls between mileposts 11 and 12 on Vermilion River Road No. 154. The trailhead and the falls are located on Plum Creek property.

Trail Length: 100 yards

Trail Condition: fair, rather steep

Elevation Gain: about 150 feet descent

Estimated Duration of Hike: 5 minutes

Sweat Index: easy

Best Features: beautiful, cascading waterfall

Availability of Water Along the Trail: trail ends by the Vermilion River

Stream Crossings: none

What's it like? When traveling the Vermilion River Road on a sunny summer day with the window down, you cannot help but hear the roar of Vermilion Falls as you approach. The falls can be seen from the road, but the short hike down a steep trail is well worth making the stop. The falls are comprised of a series of rambunctious cascades, pools and plunges for several hundred feet.

Camping: not really

Precautions: You can easily hop out onto rocks at the river's edge, but beware of slippery surfaces.

Vermilion Peak

Trail: Cabinet Divide

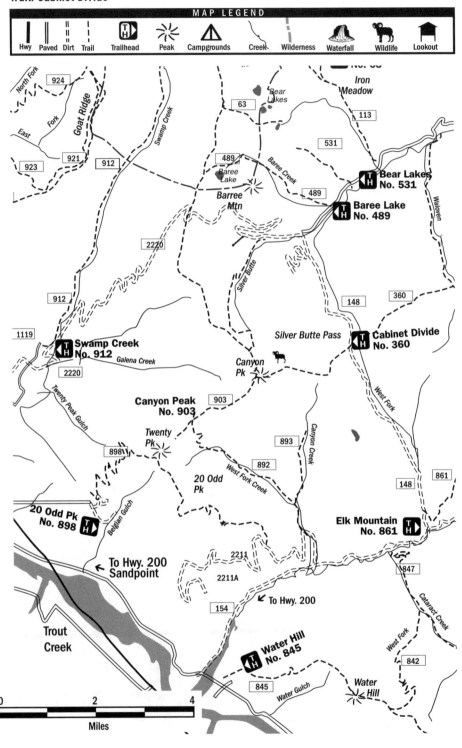

MAP LEGEND

Hwy | Paved | Dirt | Trail | Trailhead | Peak | Campgrounds | Creek | Wilderness | Waterfall | Wildlife | Lookout

924

North Fork

East Fork

Goat Ridge

Swamp Creek

Bear Lakes

63

Iron Meadow

113

531

921   912

923

489

Baree Lake

Baree Creek

489

Barree Mtn

Bear Lakes No. 531

Baree Lake No. 489

Waloven

2220

Silver Butte

148   360

912

1119

Silver Butte Pass

Cabinet Divide No. 360

Swamp Creek No. 912

Galena Creek

2220

Canyon Pk

West Fork

Canyon Peak No. 903

903

Twenty Peak Gulch

Twenty Pk

898

893

892

Canyon Creek

148

861

20 Odd Pk

West Fork Creek

20 Odd Pk No. 898

Belgian Gulch

Elk Mountain No. 861

To Hwy. 200 Sandpoint ←

2211

2211A

847

154

← To Hwy. 200

Cataract Creek

Trout Creek

West Fork

842

Water Hill No. 845

Water Hill

845   Water Gulch

0   2   4

Miles

Cabinet Divide Trail No. 360

Destination: Cabinet Divide, Canyon Peak, 6,326 feet. *Map, page 134.*

USGS Map: Silver Butte Pass, Goat Peak

Trailhead: Silver Butte Pass can be reached from Highway 2 about 20 miles south of Libby, Montana. Turn west onto Silver Butte Road 148 and go about 13 miles to the pass and the trailhead. You can also turn onto the Blue Slide Road at milepost 28 on Highway 200 about 2 miles west of Trout Creek, Montana, and follow it 4 miles to Vermilion River Road No. 154. Near milepost 7 take Silver Butte Pass Road No. 148 and go 5 miles to the pass.

Trail Length: 14 miles from Silver Butte Pass to Lost Buck Pass (in the CMW), 3 miles to Canyon Peak, or about 6 miles from the pass to Allen Peak via Waloven Creek Trail No. 293.

Trail Condition: good

Elevation Gain: 2,100 feet from Silver Butte Pass to Canyon Peak; about 2,500 feet from the pass to Allen Peak.

Estimated Duration of Hike: Silver Butte Pass to Canyon Peak takes 2 to 3 hours up, 1 to 2 hours down; from the pass to Allen Peak 3 to 4 hours up, 2 to 3 hours down.

Sweat Index: strenuous

Best Features: great views of the Clark Fork Valley and the CMW

Availability of Water Along the Trail: none, though you may find a trickle in Waloven Creek on the way to Allen Peak

Stream Crossings: none

What's it like? At Silver Butte Pass, going west on this trail means a stiff climb of 1,600 feet for the first mile and a half. Once on the ridge above the East Fork of Canyon Creek, the rewards are tremendous. This area is rife with wildlife, and the mountain vistas are superb. Canyon Peak is the high point along this trail and makes a good destination for a day hike. The trail continues beyond Canyon Peak to the edge of the Cabinet Mountains Wilderness at Baree Mountain. Less than half a mile from the wilderness boundary, the trail joins the BPA powerline maintenance road that comes up out of Swamp Creek for a short distance. East from the pass the trail meanders into Waloven Creek and joins Trail No. 293, which ascends Allen Peak through a young, even-aged forest of larch and lodgepole pine.

Camping: Ridgeline camping opportunities abound along the Cabinet Divide.

Alternate Hikes: A lot of country opens up along this trail. East of the pass the trail also climbs nearly 1,600 feet before crossing a divide into Waloven Creek, where it connects with Trail 293 and an opportunity to hike to Allen Peak, 6,740 feet. Outside the wilderness, Trail 360 connects with Canyon Peak Trail 903 and Silver Butte Creek Trail 296.

Cabinet Lakes-Thompson River

Four streams labeled "rivers" flow from the interior of the Cabinet Mountains. Two of them are found in the south end of the range: the Vermilion and the Thompson. The largest of them all is Thompson River. Explorer David Thompson is generally acknowledged to have been the first white man to walk along the lower reaches of Clark's Fork of the Columbia in 1810. In his honor several mountains, a river and a town bear his name: Thompson Falls, which is the county seat for Sanders County, Montana; Thompson River, Thompson and Little Thompson peaks; and Thompson Point.

Thompson River flows south from its headwaters on Meadow Peak (6,703 feet) and McGregor Peak (5,213 feet) by way of the Thompson Lakes and McGregor Lake. Where McGregor Creek joins the Thompson just below Little Thompson Lake, the elevation is 3,382 feet. Some 45-river miles later, it makes a dash into the Clark Fork only 800 feet lower than just about where it begins. Along the way the main river collects water from Little Thompson River, West Fork Thompson River and more than 25 other named tributaries.

Looking at Mount Headley from Cube Iron Mountain on Trail No. 450

That's a lot of country drained by this one river, and though much of it has been roaded and cut over, there are still some terrific primitive hiking experiences to be had here. Wild discoveries are just waiting to be made from the crags of Mount Headley to the meadows of Mount Silcox, from the rocky pinnacles of Sundance Ridge to the National Recreation Trail climbing the boulder-strewn slopes of Baldy Mountain.

Trails: Winniemuck Creek, Vermilion-Headley, Thompson-Headley, Cabin Lake, South Four Lakes

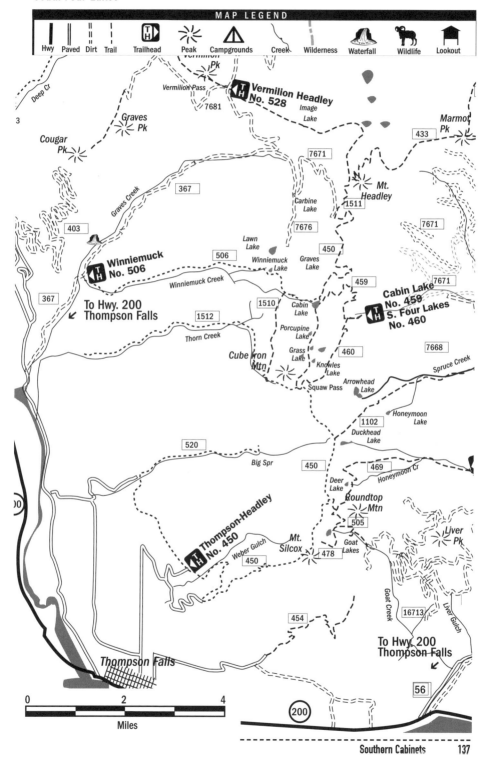

MAP LEGEND

Hwy | Paved | Dirt | Trail | Trailhead | Peak | Campgrounds | Creek | Wilderness | Waterfall | Wildlife | Lookout

Vermilion Pk

Vermilion Pass

Vermilion Headley No. 528

7681

Image Lake

Graves Pk

Cougar Pk

Deep Cr

Marmot Pk

433

7671

Mt. Headley

1511

Graves Creek

367

403

Carbine Lake

7676

450

7671

Winniemuck No. 506

Lawn Lake

Winniemuck Lake

Graves Lake

506

459

Cabin Lake No. 459

7671

367

To Hwy. 200
Thompson Falls

Winniemuck Creek

1510

Cabin Lake

S. Four Lakes No. 460

1512

Thorn Creek

Porcupine Lake

7668

Cube Iron Mtn

Grass Lake

Knowles Lake

460

Spruce Creek

Squaw Pass

Arrowhead Lake

Honeymoon Lake

1102

Duckhead Lake

520

Big Spr

450

469

Honeymoon Cr

Deer Lake

Roundtop Mtn

505

Liver Pk

Thompson-Headley No. 450

Weber Gulch

450

Mt. Silcox

478

Goat Lakes

454

Goat Creek

16713

Liver Gulch

To Hwy. 200
Thompson Falls

Thompson Falls

56

0   2   4

Miles

200

Winniemuck Creek Trail No. 506

Destination: Winniemuck Lake, Cabin Lake. *Map, page 137.*

USGS Map: Mount Headley

Trailhead: A mile west of Thompson Falls, Montana, turn off Highway 200 north onto the Blue Slide Road and follow it about 7 miles to Graves Creek Road 367. Turn northeast and go just over 2 miles to the trailhead right where the road first crosses Graves Creek on a bridge.

Trail Length: 6 miles one-way

Trail Condition: fair to good

Elevation Gain: 3,700 feet

Estimated Duration of Hike: 4 to 5 hours up, 3 to 4 hours down

Sweat Index: strenuous

Best Features: high mountain lake

Availability of Water Along the Trail: The trail closely follows Winniemuck Creek much of the way.

Stream Crossings: At times the trail is almost right in the creek.

What's it like? A long, steady climb through heavy timber characterizes a lot of this trail. But once into the glaciated cirques that pockmark the high country, the hiking is much easier and more scenic. The trail passes by

Winniemuck Lake

Winniemuck Lake, a small, shallow pothole surrounded by a dark spruce and fir forest at about 6,200 feet. From there it ascends into a narrow saddle, which looks down into the glorious basin cradling Cabin Lake. The scenery is spectacular and the subalpine forest is primeval.

Camping: Several primitive campsites are located at Cabin Lake.

Alternate Hikes: Trail 1510 joins Trail 506 at the saddle above Cabin Lake. It bears south to Cube Iron Mountain. At Cabin Lake this trail ties in with trail 450, which goes south to Squaw Pass and north to Mount Headley.

Vermilion-Headley Trail No. 528

Destination: Mount Headley, 7,429 feet. *Map, page 137.*

USGS Map: Vermilion Peak, Mount Headley

Trailhead: A mile west of Thompson Falls, Montana, turn off Highway 200 north onto the Blue Slide Road and follow it about 7 miles to Graves Creek Road 367. Take Graves Creek Road 367 all the way to Vermilion Pass. A spur road branches off to the east, but it has a small turnaround, so it is best to park on the pass and walk the road to the trail's actual beginning.

Trail Length: 4 miles one-way

Trail Condition: good

Elevation Gain: 1,400 feet

Estimated Duration of Hike: 2 to 3 hours up, 2 to 3 hours down

Sweat Index: moderate

Best Features: fantastic mountain views

Availability of Water Along the Trail: none

Stream Crossings: none

What's it like? From Vermilion Pass a road cuts across the south slope of the ridge for about a mile before becoming a trail. The trail sneaks onto the ridgeline from time to time and presents great views of Image Lake basin and the headwaters of the Vermilion River, then ducks onto the south side of a steep unnamed mountain in fairly heavy timber. Glimpses of Mount Headley are enjoyed along the way until the trail turns south and follows the ridge to the summit. Mount Headley is an awesome peak with an impressive ridge running northeast that is flanked by sheer cliffs. Another ridge characterized by steep walls on its east face points the way to a couple of small lakes high in the West Fork of Fishtrap Creek, but the terrain is rough and caution should be exercised when heading out cross-country in this region. The views from the top of Mount Headley are magnificent.

Alternate Hikes: This trail connects to a system of trails that converges on Mount Headley, including Trail 1511 from upper Graves Creek, Trail 433 from Sundance Ridge and the Thompson River and Trail 450, which begins almost 15 miles to the south in Weber Gulch just outside of Thompson Falls.

Thompson-Headley Trail No. 450

Destination: Mount Silcox, 6,854 feet. *Map, page 137.*

USGS Map: Thompson Falls, Mount Headley

Trailhead: On Highway 200 in downtown Thompson Falls, Montana, turn north opposite the Town Pump gas station and follow the signs to the Forest Service Work Center. To get there, cross the tracks and bear right on Preston Avenue, go several blocks, then turn left on Ferry Street. Go uphill several blocks (you will pass the junior high school) and turn left on Fourth, go 2 blocks and turn right on Columbia. Each of these turns is well signed. Columbia makes a jog to the left, then proceed 2 miles beyond the Forest Service Work Center to the trailhead in Weber Gulch.

Trail Length: 5 miles one-way

Trail Condition: good

Elevation Gain: 3,700 feet

Estimated Duration of Hike: 3 to 4 hours up, 2 to 3 hours down

Sweat Index: strenuous

Best Features: views of the Clark Fork River and town of Thompson Falls

Availability of Water Along the Trail: none after crossing Weber Gulch in the first half-mile

Stream Crossings: one easy crossing

What's it like? You will love the way this trail starts out so gentle and easy in a nice stand of ponderosa pine and Douglas fir. But as soon as it crosses Weber Gulch, the climb begins, and it is a dandy. The trail eventually finds the southwest shoulder of Mount Silcox, then switchbacks a zillion times until it is finally within about 200 vertical feet of the top. Some beautiful old ponderosa pines can be seen along this route. Though this hike is challenging, it offers matchless views of Thompson Falls and the Clark Fork River. High on Silcox, the ridge is typically dominated with spectacular alpine meadows and from the north end of the summit, there are fabulous views of the three Goat Lakes, Roundtop Mountain (6,858 feet) and the peaks and ridges stretching north to the Vermilion Divide.

Camping: Primitive campsites can be found beyond Mount Silcox in the nearby Goat Lakes basin.

Alternate Hikes: Trail 450 does not end at Mount Silcox; it carries on for another 9 or 10 miles through the Four Lakes Basin and up to Mount Headley, the highest peak in the area. Numerous other trails tie in along the way, including Trail 478 to Goat Lakes just northwest of the summit of Silcox. Only a couple hundred yards from the trailhead is a junction with Squaw Creek Trail No. 520, which heads northwest into Squaw Creek where it dead ends after about 6 miles.

Cabin Lake Trail No. 459
and South Four Lakes Creek Trail No. 460

Destination: Cabin Lake and Four Lakes Basin. *Map, page 137.*

USGS Map: Mount Headley

Trailhead: About 5 miles east of Thompson Falls, Montana, turn northeast onto Thompson River Road and go approximately 6 miles to the West Fork Thompson River Road No. 603. Follow that about 8 miles to the trailhead at the end of the road.

Trail Length: About 2.5 miles one-way to Cabin Lake via Trail 459 and about 2.5 miles one-way to Squaw Pass via Trail 460, thence about a mile into Four Lakes Basin.

Trail Conditions: good

Elevation Gain: 1,200 feet

Estimated Duration of Hike: from 1 to 5 hours one-way, depending on destination

Sweat Index: moderate

Best Features: beautiful alpine lakes, rugged mountain terrain

Availability of Water Along the Trail: Four Lakes Creek flows parallel to Trail 460 much of the way. There is no water along trail 459 until arriving at Cabin Lake.

Cabin Lake

Stream Crossings: A sturdy footbridge at the trailhead aids the only major stream crossing; otherwise, there are several small streams to cross.

What's it like? The Four Lakes trail system provides a terrific loop hike of about 8 miles. You have your choice at the trailhead whether to head for Cabin Lake first then the Four Lakes Basin, or hike up to Squaw Pass then drop into the basin and hike out past Cabin Lake. Either way, this is magnificent country to hike through. The lay of the land is highly interesting as it appears huge slabs of ice must have sat here for eons sculpting the terrain of this high country. When the glaciers finally melted, they left all these small lakes nestled in their alpine cirques surrounded by jagged cliffs. You might find yourself asking why the stream draining this area is called Four Lakes Creek when there are actually eight lakes and tiny potholes here, if you include Cabin Lake and its two small siblings. Taking the trail via Squaw Pass is also the easiest way to get to the summit of Cube Iron Mountain, 7,179 feet.

Camping: This basin is popular for overnight stays, so impacts from campers have been significant. Numerous primitive campsites can be found near most of the lakes.

Alternate Hikes: The access from the Four Lakes trailhead presents all kinds of hiking opportunities into the proposed Cube Iron-Silcox Wilderness.

Trails: Big Spruce Creek, Honeymoon Creek, Sundance Ridge

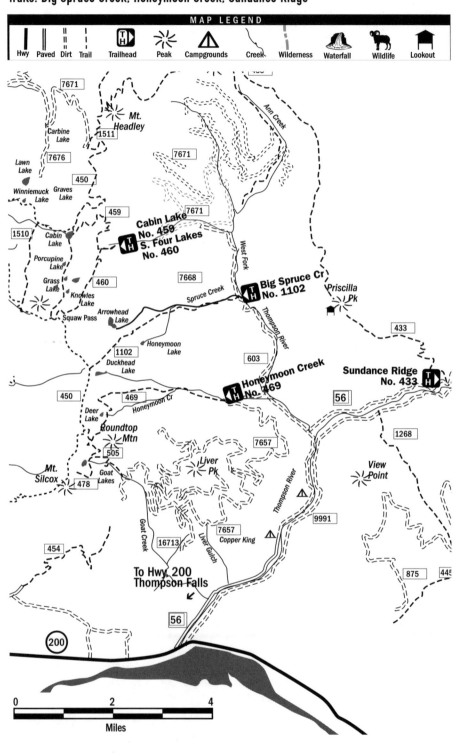

MAP LEGEND

Hwy | Paved | Dirt | Trail | Trailhead | Peak | Campgrounds | Creek | Wilderness | Waterfall | Wildlife | Lookout

7671

Mt. Headley
1511

Carbine Lake

7676

Lawn Lake

450

Winniemuck Lake | Graves Lake

459

7671

7671

Cabin Lake No. 459
S. Four Lakes No. 460

1510

Cabin Lake

Porcupine Lake

460

7668

Grass Lake

Knowles Lake

Spruce Creek

Big Spruce Cr No. 1102

Priscilla Pk

West Fork

Arrowhead Lake

Squaw Pass

433

Honeymoon Lake

1102

Duckhead Lake

Thompson River

603

Sundance Ridge No. 433

Honeymoon Creek No. 469

450

469

Honeymoon Cr

56

Deer Lake

Roundtop Mtn

7657

1268

505

Mt. Silcox

478

Goat Lakes

Liver Pk

View Point

Thompson River

9991

Goat Creek

7657

Copper King

454

16713

Liver Gulch

To Hwy 200
Thompson Falls

875

445

56

200

0   2   4
Miles

Big Spruce Creek Trail No. 1102

Destination: Arrowhead Lake, Duckhead Lake. *Map, page 142.*

USGS Map: Mount Headley, Priscilla Peak

Trailhead: About 5 miles east of Thompson Falls, Montana, turn northeast onto Thompson River Road and go approximately 6 miles to the West Fork Thompson River Road No. 603. Take it nearly 4 miles, and look for the trailhead at the Big Spruce Creek crossing.

Trail Length: 3 miles to Arrowhead Lake, 4 miles to Duckhead Lake, 4.5 miles to the junction with Trail No. 450

Trail Condition: good

Elevation Gain: 3,100 feet to the junction of Trail 450

Estimated Duration of Hike: 3 to 4 hours up, 2 to 3 hours down

Sweat Index: strenuous

Best Features: high mountain lakes, ridgeline hiking

Availability of Water Along the Trail: Water is readily available most of the way.

Stream Crossings: The trail crosses Big Spruce Creek a couple of times, but the crossings are no trouble.

What's it like? In heavy timber virtually all the way, this trail closely follows Big Spruce Creek until it climbs into the basin harboring Arrowhead Lake. A spur trail accesses the lake to the north. South of the trail is a low, steep-sided ridge over which is a small gem of a lake called Honeymoon Lake. About a mile past Arrowhead, the trail switchbacks up a hillside to a saddle and continues west to the main divide and its junction with trail 450. In that saddle it is possible to drop into Duckhead Lake about 400 feet below with a bit of bushwhacking. If you are wondering about the name, "Duckhead," take a look at it on a map and see if you can discern the shape of a duck's head.

Camping: Several primitive campsites are located near the lakes along this trail.

Alternate Hikes: This trail connects to Trail 450 on the ridgeline above Duckhead Lake, which in turn joins Honeymoon Creek Trail No. 469. These 3 trails make for a great open loop hike of about 15 miles.

Honeymoon Creek Trail No. 469

Destination: Deer Lake, Goat Lakes. *Map, page 142.*

USGS Map: Mount Headley, Priscilla Peak

Trailhead: About 5 miles east of Thompson Falls, Montana, turn northeast onto Thompson River Road and go approximately 6 miles to the West Fork Thompson River Road No. 603. Proceed almost 2 miles and turn west onto Honeymoon Creek Road 7657 and go just over a mile to the trailhead.

Trail Length: 3 miles one-way to Deer Lake, 4.5 miles one-way to Goat Lakes

Trail Condition: good

Elevation Gain: 2,600 feet to Deer Lake, 3,300 feet to the junction of Trail 450

Estimated Duration of Hike: 2 to 3 hours to Deer Lake, 3 to 4 hours to Goat Lakes, from 2 to 3 hours back down

Sweat Index: strenuous

Best Features: high mountain lakes, rugged mountain scenery

Availability of Water Along the Trail: Honeymoon Creek is close to the trail at the beginning, but after about a mile and a half it climbs the mountainside, and there is no water until Deer Lake.

Stream Crossings: A couple of crossings pose no serious obstacle.

What's it like? During the first mile or so, this trail hugs Honeymoon Creek, crossing it then re-crossing it before starting up the ridge between the forks flowing from Deer Lake and Duckhead Lake. The elevation gain is pretty strenuous for about 2 miles, as the trail climbs some 2,500 feet through mostly dense forest. The trail meanders through a beautiful, small basin, curves around to the south, then heaves over a ridge into Deer Lake. The view of the lake coming in over that ridge is awesome. For nearly a mile beyond the lake, the trail winds farther into the basin and comes to a junction with Goat Lakes Connector Trail No. 505. It climbs a couple of hundred feet over a ridge just west of Roundtop Mountain (6,858 feet) and drops into the Goat Lakes Basin.

Camping: Primitive campsites can be found at each of the lakes accessed by these trails.

Alternate Hikes: This trail connects to Trail 450 on the ridgeline between Mt. Silcox and Squaw Pass. Also near the top, Trail 505 takes off into the Goat Lakes basin. A variety of open-loop hikes are possible using these trails.

Sundance Ridge Trail No. 433

Destination: Priscilla Peak, 7,005 feet, Marmot Peak, 7,200 feet, Mount Headley, 7,429 feet. *Map, page 142.*

USGS Map: Priscilla Peak, Mount Headley

Trailhead: About 5 miles east of Thompson Falls, Montana, turn northeast onto Thompson River Road and stay on the west side of the river on the county road (don't take what is often called the Champion Haul Road). Proceed to about the 9-mile marker and the trailhead.

Trail Length: 4 miles one-way to Priscilla Peak Lookout, 10 miles one-way to Marmot Peak, 14 miles one-way to Mount Headley

Trail Condition: fair to good

Elevation Gain: 4,300 feet to Priscilla Peak Lookout

Estimated Duration of Hike: 3 to 4 hours to Priscilla Peak, 5 to 6 hours to Marmot Peak, 7 to 9 hours to Mount Headley

Sweat Index: strenuous

Best Features: old lookout tower available for rent, excellent mountain views

Availability of Water Along the Trail: A small spring emerges just above the trail a mile north of Priscilla Peak Lookout.

Stream Crossings: none

What's it like? Be prepared for a heck of a climb for the first couple of miles up this trail as it switchbacks endlessly above the Thompson River. The forest is relatively open, and views of the river are nice. Some beautiful open meadows greet the hiker higher up the mountainside, and wonderful vistas looking right down the Thompson River to the Clark Fork valley follow you the rest of the way to the lookout. Priscilla Peak is a round knob draped with rocks and grassy meadows and scattered trees. From here the trail actually drops into the upper basins of Deerhorn Creek before regaining the ridge, which it then follows out over Marmot Peak. Then it drops precipitously into one of the many small lakes feeding the West Fork of Fishtrap Creek. The ascent up out of this basin to Mount Headley is a doozy, but the scenery is superb. Inspiring cliffs wrap around this glacial cirque, which seems as wild as any place on earth.

Camping: The lookout tower atop Priscilla Peak is available for rent, but it is a rustic setting with no amenities other than an enclosed roof over your head. Contact the Plains Ranger Station for details.

Alternate Hikes: Trail 433 carries all the way out to Mount Headley. Several other trails connect to this one along the way, including Trail 167 from Beatrice Creek. The junctions of old trails 426 and 427 in the Marmot Peak area are evident but they have been abandoned and are no longer maintained. The same goes for Deer Creek Trail No. 260 several miles north of Priscilla Peak. A good set of topographic maps is recommended for the hike along trail 433.

Trail: Munson Creek

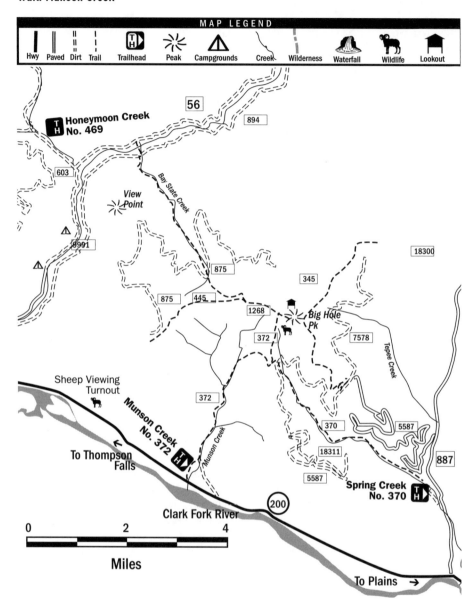

MAP LEGEND

| Hwy | Paved | Dirt | Trail | Trailhead | Peak | Campgrounds | Creek | Wilderness | Waterfall | Wildlife | Lookout |

Honeymoon Creek No. 469

56

894

603

Bay State Creek

View Point

8991

875

345

18300

875   445

1268

Big Hole Pk

372

7578

372

Tepee Creek

Sheep Viewing Turnout

Munson Creek No. 372

372

370

5587

To Thompson Falls

Munson Creek

18311

887

5587

Spring Creek No. 370

Clark Fork River

200

0   2   4

Miles

To Plains →

Munson Creek Trail No. 372

Destination: Big Hole Peak, 6,922 feet. *Map, page 146.*

USGS Map: Big Hole Peak

Trailhead: A quarter mile east of milepost 62 on Highway 200 about 13 miles west of Plains, Montana, the highway crosses Munson Creek. An obscure dirt road turns north off the highway perhaps a couple of hundred yards east of the creek crossing and next to an old, unoccupied cabin. The road switchbacks once up a hill to the trailhead parking area a hundred yards or so from the highway.

Trail Length: 6 miles one-way

Trail Condition: fair to good

Elevation Gain: 4,500 feet

Estimated Duration of Hike: 4 to 5 hours up, 3 to 4 hours down

Sweat Index: strenuous

Best Features: forest fire lookout, evidence of forest fires, fabulous mountain and valley views, wildlife (bighorn sheep)

Availability of Water Along the Trail: The trail parallels Munson Creek for several miles.

Stream Crossings: 3 easy crossings

What's it like? A pleasant stroll through a forest of ponderosa pines characterizes the start of this hike. Most of the first mile is on an old jeep track, but once the track enters the Munson Creek Canyon below some spectacular cliffs, look for the trail to take off to the left above the road. Once in the canyon notice the excessively worn game trails crisscrossing Trail 372. Bighorn sheep have created these trails, and it is possible to see sheep in the heavy timber along the lower slopes just above the stream. A couple of miles up the trail, evidence of past forest fires becomes apparent. Some of the burned areas were torched intentionally to enhance wildlife habitat. On the higher slopes panoramic vistas open up where lodgepole pine has either burned or been killed by bark beetles, and the resulting meadows and brush fields are now prime habitat for mule deer and elk. At the summit of Big Hole Peak is a forest fire lookout structure and magnificent views of the Clark Fork Valley and the south end of the Cabinet Mountains.

Camping: A primitive campsite is located near the third stream crossing about 3 miles up the trail. Camping on the mountaintop near the lookout can be spectacular, but keep in mind you will need to pack water.

Alternate Hikes: Spring Creek Trail No. 370 joins this trail about 2 miles from the top of Big Hole Peak; Trail No. 535 is a connecting trail linking Trail 372 with Trail No. 368; and near the peak Trail 372 ties in with Bay State Creek Trail No. 1268, which comes out in Thompson River to the northwest. Several excellent open-loop hikes are possible on Big Hole Peak.

Trail: Baldy National Recreation

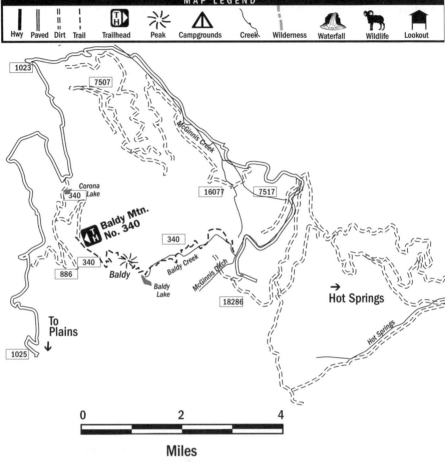

MAP LEGEND

| Hwy | Paved | Dirt | Trail | Trailhead | Peak | Campgrounds | Creek | Wilderness | Waterfall | Wildlife | Lookout |

1023
7507
McGinnis Creek
Corona Lake
340
16077
7517
Baldy Mtn. No. 340
340
340
886
Baldy
Baldy Creek
McGinnis Ditch
Baldy Lake
18286
→ Hot Springs
Hot Springs
To Plains ↓
1025

0   2   4

Miles

Baldy Lake

Baldy National Recreation Trail No. 340

Destination: Baldy Mountain, 7,464 feet and Baldy Lake. *Map, page 148.*

USGS Map: Baldy Lake

Trailhead: A half-mile northwest of Plains, Montana, turn east off Highway 200 and go past the hospital to a T-junction. Turn north and follow this paved road to Cedar Creek Road. Take the left fork, which is a gravel road. Follow the signs for Corona Road until you come to the junction of Road 886 about 4 miles after the Cedar Creek fork. There is a sign for the trailhead, which is just over 3 miles from there at the end of the road.

Trail Length: 2 miles one-way to Baldy Mountain, 3 miles one-way to the lake

Trail Condition: good

Elevation Gain: 1,500 feet to the summit, then 700 feet down to the lake

Estimated Duration of Hike: 1 to 2 hours up, and 1 to 2 hours down, an additional hour each way to the lake

Sweat Index: difficult

Best Features: spectacular views of the Clark Fork Valley, beautiful mountain lake

Availability of Water Along the Trail: none

Stream Crossings: none

What's it like? Baldy is a big mountain, but this trail has its beginning at about 6,000 feet, so the climb is not overwhelming. The first couple of hundred yards is along an old roadbed, which then joins up with the trail. The trail slants downhill and ties in with Road 886 about a mile and a half before the end-of-the-road trailhead, as well as continuing toward the summit. Proceed uphill to get to the top. Look for mule deer in the clear-cut screened by a line of timber just down slope. The trail traverses a forest of Douglas fir, larch and lodgepole pine, but soon the others give way and lodgepole and whitebark pine dominate the high, windswept mountainside. Take note of the unusual twisted shapes of many of the trees, illustrating the harsh nature of the environment in which they are growing. The final mile to the summit is achieved by way of one switchback after another across broken talus rock. The views in all directions are increasingly fabulous the higher you go. At the top, which is a broad, rounded summit, are the remains of an old lookout. The trail goes right over the peak and starts down the east side toward the lake about 700 vertical feet below. The lake is walled on one side by spectacular cliffs on its southern shoreline.

Camping: There is several places to camp near the lake.

Alternate Hikes: Trail 340 continues east from Baldy Lake to McGinnis Creek for about 2 miles.

Glacious

Carefully picking our way through the dark timber, we followed what we assumed to be the trail near the base of a talus slope. Though it was the last day of June and summer was 10 full days upon us, snow lay 5 or 6 feet deep in the high basin tucked in close to Cube Iron Mountain's shadowy northeast slope. Only some hatchet blazes about 6 feet up the trunk of an occasional tree – just about at snow depth level – indicated we were on course.

Archie, my oldest brother, three nephews and I wended our way along a rocky bench, through a swale full of snow and out onto an avalanche chute. Mangled trees caught up in the frozen mass that had come crashing down off the windswept ridge above angled crazily out of the snow like splintered toothpicks. Cube Iron's starkly silhouetted summit pierced the angry sky across which clouds scuttled like flaming race cars in the late afternoon glow of the setting sun.

The spectacle was awesome. The five of us stood in reverent silence, captivated by this wintry scene on the eve of July as idiotic smiles of wild ecstasy played on each face. These guys, all from back east, were not accustomed to such a landscape, I mused, and it was easy to see in their eyes the awe they felt for the magnificent terrain surrounding us.

Then from out of the hushed stillness of this alpine cirque, from which I would not have been surprised to hear the voice of God, there came an exclamation of delight from my nephew, Matt. "Glacious!" he cried, then laughed out loud. We all echoed the phrase, and we strode across the remnants of winter's avalanche in search of the trail to the ridge top.

Glacious. I have since used the word coined by Matt that day elsewhere in the mountains to summarize the feelings of delight I have experienced when in the high country. But few trips into the mountains have delighted me as much as those three days with Tim, Matt, Dan and Archie. Sharing the raw energy that seeps into my soul every time I venture into the mountains with family was a rare treat.

We had begun this hike at Winniemuck Creek just a mile below Graves Creek Falls. From the trailhead it is a steady climb to the land called the Cabinet Lakes Country. Six miles and several thousand feet of elevation got us to Cabin Lake and the site of our first night's camp. We were hard pressed to find a dry, snow-less patch of ground for the tents. A hearty campfire handed each of us a smile, though, and the lingering winter did not diminish the joys we spoke of well into the night.

For me the joy was as simple as being in a wild place cooking supper over a campfire, gazing at the stars and huddling closer to the flames to ward off the evening's chill – sharing the moment with those with whom I share a bloodline.

None of my three nephews were born before I left Virginia for the Montana Rockies. That fact has meant I have seen them infrequently and missed out on the privilege of watching them grow. And that fact has left an empty spot inside me that nothing else has ever filled. Those three days on the trail, though, took us all down a path which led to a little better understanding of what makes us tick.

Perhaps we discovered that what fundamentally makes any of us tick is the same power, the exact same energy, that put Cube Iron Mountain in place; that force which dictates water flows downhill; the same mysterious sovereignty that guides the stars through the dark night sky; the same sapient will that binds the threads of brotherhood into an even stronger knot of human compassion. And then, perhaps we ingenuously discovered that it was nothing more than a whole lot of fun hiking and camping in the mountains with people you like.

Our second day on the trail took us into the heart of the Cabinet Lakes Country, and we skirted past Porcupine, Frog, Grass and Knowles lakes. The silence of the snow-enshrouded forest was deafening. The only sound was the crunching of our footsteps across the crusty snow. Then we came to the avalanche chute, and the surprised yell that swept us all into a euphoric cry of "Glacious!" and fits of laughter at the silliness of it.

A tedious ascent greeted us in the dark timber on the other side of the avalanche. The trail had entirely disappeared beneath the thick mantle of snow, so we faced uphill, craning our necks in order to fix our gaze on the cornice stitched across the ridgeline like a satin lace on the hem of a garment. Squaw Pass was up there somewhere, and we needed to find it and a way over this mountain. All that could be done was to plant our toes deep into the snow and climb.

Gray clouds had gathered in the west; it was as if attaining the top of the ridge opened a gate, and they came tumbling across the sky in a rush. Gale-force winds gusted over the shoulder of Cube Iron, and swirling mists engulfed its ragged head. Crystals of snow and slanted rain rode the icy blasts in a frenzy of madness. Moments of panic nearly overran us as we searched for some sheltered enclave in which to pitch camp.

The nerve shattering worries that we were going to be blown from the mountain back into the darkening hollow from which we had emerged passed with a single ray of sunshine. We discovered shelter beneath the protective limbs of several gnarly trees and a trickle of snowmelt from an overhanging drift to ensure enough water for hot drinks and a hot meal that evening.

Our campfire danced crazily with the gyrating air currents into the night. We drew close – as close as the spitting embers and exploding sparks would allow – and soaked up the warmth of the flames and, more so, the warmth of camaraderie.

The next day saw us cross over Cube Iron Mountain and descend Thorne Creek back to the road and a truck. We were tired, we were elated, and each of us, in our own way, I think, understood better than anyone at precisely that moment how to express the delight the wilderness instills when you are willing to explore the depths of mankind's connection to the land ... glacious!

Appendix A:

Trails Suitable for Mountain Bikes

A friend of mine who loves to get out in the woods, breathe fresh air, soak up the scenery and seek solitude in the wild backcountry enjoys his time outdoors a little differently than I. He says, "Dennis, why hike it when you can bike it?"

The Cabinet Mountains offer unparalleled opportunities for mountain bikers on a system of open and closed roads that cover thousands of miles, not to mention the off-road routes that beckon hardcore riders to experience the greatest challenges of all – single track trails that will test the strength of the strongest riders. A lot of the trails described in this hiking guide will accommodate mountain bikes, but be warned: Trail riding in the Cabinets can be extremely difficult and dangerous. These trails are not maintained with mountain bikes in mind.

Also remember this: Mountain bikes are prohibited in the Cabinet Mountains Wilderness. Some trails leading up to the wilderness boundary are suitable for bikes, but never go beyond the boundary. At all times take the utmost precaution when traveling a trail on a bike and be prepared for any circumstance. The potential for soaring headfirst over the handlebars is pretty high. And finally, share the trail. More and more people are discovering the great recreational opportunities that abound in the Cabinets and there is plenty of room for us all. Whether hiking, biking, on horseback or cruising the backcountry in winter on snowshoes or skis, it only takes common courtesy on everyone's part to ensure everyone enjoys their visit into the Wild Cabinets.

With all this in mind, below is the list of trails described in this guide and just how bikeable they may be for an experienced mountain biker.

Cabinet Mountains Wilderness (remember, no bikes in the wilderness, but pedaling to the wilderness boundary is acceptable in most cases)

The North End: William Grambauer Mountain to Flower Creek

William Grambauer Mountain Trail No. 319	extreme
Scenery Mountain Trail No. 649	extreme
Cedar Lakes Trail No. 141	difficult
Taylor Peak Trail No. 320	extreme
Dome Mountain Trail No. 360	prohibited
Minor Lake Trail No. 317	prohibited
Parmenter Creek Trail No. 140	difficult
Flower Creek/Sky Lakes Trail No. 137	difficult
Hanging Valley Trail No. 135	prohibited

The Central CMW: Granite Creek to Rock Lake

Crowell Creek	moderately difficult
North Fork Bull River Trail No. 972	moderate

A forest road offers a couple of miles of riding to the trailhead, along with about 2 miles of trail before encountering the wilderness boundary.

Middle Fork Bull River Trail No. 978   moderately difficult
A short section of forest road accesses the trailhead, and again there is only about 2 miles of trail before encountering the wilderness boundary.

Little Ibex Lake Trail No. 980   prohibited
Moderately difficult to the falls; prohibited beyond that.

Granite Lake Trail No. 136   difficult

Leigh Lake Trail No. 132   difficult

Dad Peak Trail No. 966   extreme

St. Paul Lake Trail No. 646   prohibited

Moran Basin Trail No. 993   moderately easy
11 miles of closed road offer a great ride to the trailhead for trail 993. Views of the Bull River valley are fantastic.

Rock Lake Trail No. 935   moderately easy
Nearly 3 miles along an old mining road offer a terrific ride to the site of the historic Heidelberg Mine. The single-track trail beyond this point is extreme.

Trail to Cliff Lake   prohibited

Berray Mountain West Trail No. 967   difficult
5 miles of trail climb steeply up this mountainside and the trail does not enter the wilderness. But this would be a tough ride.

Berray Mountain Trail No. 1028   moderately difficult
This trail does not enter the wilderness, but its 2.5 miles contains a couple of steep pitches on the way to the old lookout.

The South End: Engle Lake to Baree Lake

Engle Lake Trail No. 932   extreme

Engle Peak Trail No. 926   extreme

Wanless Lake Trail No. 924   difficult
Trail 924 climbs 7 miles to a pass west of Goat Peak and the wilderness boundary, butbefore reaching the pass, Goat Ridge Trail 921 heads south to its junction with Bearpaw Trail 923, which goes back to the same trailhead parking area as for Trail 924. These three trails make for about a 14-mile loop that would be a difficult but interesting challenge for many mountain bikers.

Swamp Creek Trail No. 912   difficult

Bramlet Lake Trail No. 658   easy
An old mining road accesses this lake 1.5 miles from the trailhead. The wilderness boundary is less than 100 yards from the lake.

Geiger Lakes Trail 656   moderately difficult
There is about 2 miles of trail before the wilderness boundary.

Divide Cutoff Trail No. 63   extreme
See explanation for Cabinet Divide Trail No. 360 in the Vermilion-Fisher River section of the South Cabinets, page 154. Remember – no bikes on the wilderness portion of this trail.

Iron Meadow Trail No. 113   moderate
This is a highly rideable trail outside the wilderness that connects both with trails leading into the wilderness and other trails traversing the terrain adjacent to the southeast end of the CMW. Some excellent biking opportunities can be found here.

Bear Lakes Trail No. 531   difficult

Baree Lake Trail No. 489   difficult

Divide Cutoff Trail No. 63   difficult

West Cabinets

Katka-Boulder

Katka Peak Trail No. 182   moderately difficult
From the trailhead west of Clifty Mountain, this trail provides a terrific biking opportunity all the way out to Katka Peak, about 5 miles.

McGinty Ridge Trail No. 143   extreme

Iron Mountain Trail No. 180   extreme

Buck Mountain Trail No. 176   extreme

East Fork Boulder Creek Trail No. 136   moderately easy
From near Boulder City this trail (an old road bed for several miles) affords a good ride to where it crosses Road 688, which can then be taken to the main road and back to the ghost town for a fine loop ride of about 12 miles.

Timber Mountain Trail No. 51   easy to difficult
From the trailhead at the end of Road 427 in upper Boulder Creek, this trail follows the old roadbed from Boulder Meadows to Callahan Divide (a distance of about 5 miles). From there take your choice of following Trail 51 to its junction with Trail 548 and down it into North Callahan Creek and on to Troy, or take Pend Oreille Divide Trail 67 to Calder Mountain and beyond for as far as you want to go, or head down Trail 488 into Grouse Creek. A great loop is also feasible by following the Orville Heath Trail 54 to Bald Eagle Mountain, then down Kelly Pass Trail 155 back to Boulder Creek.

Kelly Pass Trail No. 155   moderately difficult
See comments above for Timber Mountain Trail 51.

Orville Heath Trail No. 54   moderately difficult
See comments above for Timber Mountain Trail 51.

North Callahan Trail No. 548   moderately difficult
See comments above for Timber Mountain Trail 51.

Pend Oreille Divide

Pend Oreille Divide Trail No. 67   moderately difficult
This ridgeline trail offers some great biking on what is sometimes a tough tread for bikes, but the grade is usually gentle and the views are fabulous.

Lake Darling Trail No. 52   easy
An excellent short ride to the lake, or go farther to the divide and try to make the top of Pend Oreille Mountain.

Gem Lake Trail No. 554   difficult

Moose Lake Trail No. 237   easy
Another excellent short ride to a lake and beautiful scenery.

Blacktail Lake Trail No. 24   moderately difficult
The trail to Blacktail Lake takes off from the Moose Lake trail and climbs steadily over the shoulder of Moose Mountain and down into the lake basin. There are a lot of boardwalks over marshy areas, so this might not be a trail very suitable for bikes.

Lake Estelle Trail No. 36   moderately difficult
This trail also takes off from the Moose Lake trail and climbs through a pass and along a steep, rocky mountainside to the lake.

Bee Top-Round Top Trail No. 120   moderately difficult
The place to start out on this trail is at its north end on the saddle between Trestle and Lightning creeks. The total length of the trail is nearly 20 miles, so you can go as far as you want. Good access can also be had from Wellington Creek Road No. 489.

Bee Top Trail No. 63   moderately difficult
Once on the ridgeline this trail offers a nice ride out to Bee Top, though the tread is often rocky and uneven.

Strong Creek Trail No. 444   moderately difficult

One of the more popular mountain biking trails in the region is this old road up Strong Creek to the top of the ridge near Round Top. The Bee Top-Round Top Trail crosses this path at the summit and offers the biker several opportunities for some terrific hardcore biking either toward Trestle Creek or down the Wellington Creek Road into Lightning Creek or southeast along the ridge to Bee Top Trail No. 63.

Scotchman Peaks

Little Spar Lake Trail No. 143   extreme

Ross Creek Nature Trail No. 405   easy to difficult

The Ross Creek Cedars Nature Trail is an easy short loop, or you can follow Trail 142 beyond the cedar grove farther upstream. The going gets much more difficult and the forks of the trail both dead-end after several miles.

Pillick Ridge Trail No. 1036   extreme

Dry Creek Tie-in Trail No. 1018   easy

Except for a few stream crossings, this trail is a pleasant ride through a thick forest for several miles. It connects to three other trails, two of which go to Squaw Peak and the active forest fire lookout tower on top.

Star Gulch Trail No. 1016   difficult

This trail would be a tough climb on a bike.

Napoleon Gulch Trail No. 1035   difficult

Same with this one.

Big Eddy Trail No. 998   difficult to extreme

From Highway 200 where this trail begins as an old mining road, it is a hard, steep climb for a couple of miles to the single track, which then becomes even more difficult along its switchbacks to the top.

Blacktail Creek Trail No. 997   difficult

Hamilton Gulch Trail No. 1019   difficult

Scotchman Peak Trail No. 65   extreme

East Fork Peak Trail No. 563   extreme

Southern Cabinets

Vermilion-Fisher River

20 Odd Peak Trail No. 898   difficult

It is a steep climb for a bike along this trail's 4 miles to the top.

Canyon Peak Trail No. 903   moderately easy

Once at the top of 20 Odd, the ridge trail over Twenty Peak and out to Canyon Peak is a nice ride.

Allen Peak Trail No. 293   difficult

From Sims Creek, the ascent to Allen Peak is pretty steep, but Trail 293 makes a broad open loop that offers a challenging ride.

Moose Peak Trail No. 877   difficult

Elk Lake Trail No. 882   difficult

Elk Mountain Trail No. 861   extreme

Cataract Creek Trail No. 847   difficult

This trail forms a portion of the route for the Vermilion River Challenge Mountain Bike Race, but its 7.5 miles includes four stream crossings and a lot of rock, plus a wade across the Vermilion River.

Water Hill Trail No. 845   extreme

Vermilion-Seven Point Trail No. 528   easy to difficult

This is another portion of the single-track route for the Vermilion River Challenge. Much of this trail is easy ridge-top riding, but there is enough up and down and talus rock to make it more difficult than you might think.

| Trail to Vermilion Falls | extreme |
| Cabinet Divide Trail No. 360 | difficult |

The Cabinet Divide trail exits the wilderness' south end at Baree Mountain close to where a giant BPA power line crosses the divide, and here is where a great mountain biking opportunity awaits. By following the power line maintenance road from Swamp Creek to the top of the mountain, you can connect to Trail 360 and take it out to Canyon Peak and either continue to Silver Butte Pass or follow Trail 903 around the headwall of Galena Creek to Twenty Peak and come out the bottom on 20 Odd Mountain Trail 898.

Cabinet Lakes-Thompson River

| Winniemuck Creek Trail No. 506 | difficult |

A long steady climb to Cabin Lake.

| Vermilion-Headley Trail No. 528 | easy to difficult |

A road traverses the mountainside from Vermilion Pass to a point that overlooks the Image Lake basin, then the trail continues out to Mount Headley.

| Thompson-Headley Trail No. 450 | difficult |

The first mile of this trail will be easy on a bike, but once it starts to ascend the ridge leading to Mount Silcox it becomes much more difficult.

Cabin Lake Trail No. 459	extreme
South Four Lakes Trail No. 460	extreme
Big Spruce Creek Trail No. 1102	extreme
Honeymoon Creek Trail No. 469	extreme
Sundance Ridge Trail No. 433	extreme
Munson Creek Trail No. 372	extreme
Baldy National Recreation Trail No. 340	extreme

Updates on the suitability of trails for mountain bikes can be obtained at any Forest Service office. Check page 157 for contact information. As management of trails evolves, it is possible some of the trails mentioned here may be closed to mountain bike use or maintained to better accommodate mountain bikers.

Appendix B:

Who to Contact for Recreation Information:

Kootenai National Forest
www.fs.fed.us/r1/kootenai
Supervisor's Office
1101 U.S. Highway 2 West
Libby, MT 59923
(406) 293-6211

Three Rivers Ranger District
Troy Ranger Station
1437 North Highway 2
Troy, MT 59935
(406) 295-4693

Libby Ranger District
Canoe Gulch Ranger Station
12557 Highway 37 North
Libby, MT 59923
(406) 293-7773

Cabinet Ranger District
2693 Highway 200
Trout Creek, MT 59874
(406) 827-3533

Lolo National Forest
www.fs.fed.us/r1/lolo
Plains/Thompson Falls
Ranger District
Plains Ranger Station
408 Clayton
Plains, MT 59859
(406) 826-3821

**Idaho Panhandle
National Forests**
www.fs.fed.us/ipnf
Supervisor's Office
3815 Schreiber Way
Coeur d'Alene, ID 83815
(208) 765-7223

Bonners Ferry Ranger District
Route 4, Box 4860
Bonners Ferry, ID 83805
(208) 267-5561

Sandpoint Ranger District
1500 Highway 2, Suite 110
Sandpoint, ID 83864
(208) 263-5111

On the Internet
www.SandpointOnline.com
Lodging, access and visitor infor-
mation for the region

www.lnt.org
Site for the Leave No Trace Center
for Outdoor Ethics with informa-
tion on "leave no trace" hiking
and camping techniques

Before Columbus

Ten years. They can seem like a long time, but anymore a decade flies by. Those first 10 years, though – my first 10 years, the years of discovery, the years of youth – can seem like a lifetime. And if a decade is a lifetime, then I have lived fifty lifetimes and then some since those first ten years.

You see, 10 years before Columbus sailed the ocean blue, if the nursery rhyme about 1492 is correct, a seed germinated on a ridge above Sparrow Gulch and I was born. The first thing I remember hearing was the song of the river a quarter mile away. The canyon narrows just below here, and the Vermilion River tumbles through a gorge in a series of spectacular cascades, falls and rapids. The melody was a soothing lullaby day after day in the early years, like the voice of the land singing and laughing. It has since become a thread woven into the very fabric of my existence.

I am a tamarack, or a larch, some will call me. At the turn of the century – the new century we are now in – I turned 518 years old. I never knew Christopher Columbus, but I can tell you I was a strapping young sapling the day he "discovered" the New World.

1481 was a good seed year for larch in the Cabinet Mountains. Following some long forgotten fire, my ancestors cast a bumper crop of cones upon the land and a bunch of us seedlings sprouted a year later. We grew to be a forest in the isolated heart of the Vermilion River canyon with our cousins, the Douglas fir and pines, the cedar and cottonwoods along the river below, the spruce and sub-alpine fir on the mountaintops above.

They are all gone now, those pines and fir and spruce, and most of the larch from those days. But there are four of us left. I can see the other three from where I stand, though they likely cannot see me. Nearly a century ago I lost my top. My memory fails me, but I guess some big wind swept upriver from the big valley and snapped it like a toothpick. I am barely a hundred feet tall now.

The big fellow down below also had his top snap off years ago, but he was so huge that I can still see his limbs raking the sky. In the more fertile soil of the creek bottom he reached over 6 feet in diameter and twice the height I am now.

Farther up the slope one of the other two is having quite the struggle, and I fear we will lose him some year soon. Perhaps he is dead already. From my van-tage point I can't tell. All I see are skeletal gray branches stark against the azure summer sky.

My nearest companion appears to be in the best shape of any of us, though that doesn't really say much. He has a full, green crown, but every limb looks to be infected with mistletoe. Though he is near the ridgeline like I am, he has managed to keep his top all this time, and, by God, he is still putting on some growth.

By the time I was 115 years old, I was boasting a girth of over 50 inches. Not bad for having to tough it out in the shallow rocky soil of this mountainside. However, it has taken 400 years to add another 50 inches to my waistline. It now takes up to 10 years to add a simple one-tenth of an inch to my diameter.

It's okay, though. I reckon my friends and I ought to count ourselves lucky to still be here. A lot of younger, smaller trees have succumbed to disease or fallen to the saw and been cut into lumber. Maybe that is my fate too. Not long ago a man wrapped his measuring tape around my trunk and sunk a steel bore into my wood to see how big and old I am. I didn't feel a thing; but then, I have been on this mountain through fires and storms and bitter cold. The forest has come and gone a dozen times. Flames have scorched my bark and singed my branches. Ice has coated my trunk and snow has piled up on my head. The wind has rushed through my foliage like waters over the falls in the gorge below. But don't think I have grown numb after all these years, these decades, these five centuries plus. I am still alive.

The world is a fascinating place, even on the remote ridge from which I have surveyed it through time. I don't expect I will be here another 500 years, but where else could I have grown up and grown old that is more beautiful, more enchanting than right here, surrounded by the mountains, nourished by the river, shoulder to shoulder with my kin?

I still hear the melody of the river. Its music never stops. I never cease listening. I can't. It feeds me; it comforts me. The river and I, and the rest of the forest, are bound together by the land that cradles us like a mother protectively embracing her young. And today she hums rhythmically the same soft music that welcomed me into this world before Columbus landed on distant shores.

In that, I have found contentment for over 500 years. I will leave this world when my time comes, but the music will go on. The mountains are eternal, and I will rest here into time immemorial, at home in the heart of the Cabinets.

•••

In 1996 I was the man who bored into that larch and measured its girth as part of a timber survey for the Forest Service. The tree is still there, safe perhaps, in one of the Cabinet's wild areas that remain off limits to logging, for now.

A lot of these types of discoveries are out there to be made, in hidden valleys, across steep mountainsides and atop ridges and peaks up and down the length of this mountain range. A lot more trails than are covered in this book go to those places, but many of the best and most exciting experiences are to be made off trail. Careful planning and an adventurous spirit can lead to remarkable encounters in these mountains.

I have hiked a lot of miles in the Cabinets, but there are others who have hiked a lot more; who know the country a lot better than I. Any mistakes in the descriptions presented in this book could be because my memory of the trail fails me or maybe they are intentional because I don't really want anyone else trespassing into my most treasured secret places. So many wonderful things are to be seen, smelled and touched in the backcountry of the Cabinet Mountains. Like you, if you have read this far, I have a yearning to see, smell and touch every secret valley and every soaring peak in these mountains; to grow old in the shadow of its forests, in the moonlit aura of its meadows.

It could take a decade; maybe it would take 500 years to see it all. Perhaps it cannot be done in a lifetime. But where else could I grow old that is more beautiful, more enchanting than right here, surrounded by these mountains, nourished by their rivers, shoulder to shoulder with those who share the kindred spirit of love for places that are wild?

– Dennis Nicholls
Spring 2003

PHOTO BY ARCHIE NICHOLLS